Encyclopedia of the Animal World

BIRDS
The Plant- and Seed-Eaters

Jill Bailey & Steve Parker

Facts On File
New York • Oxford

THE PLANT- AND SEED-EATERS
The Encyclopedia of the Animal World:
Birds

Managing Editor: Lionel Bender
Art Editor: Ben White
Designer: Malcolm Smythe
Text Editor: Miles Litvinoff
Assistant Editor: Madeleine Samuel
Project Editor: Graham Bateman
Production: Clive Sparling, Joanna
   Turner

Media conversion and typesetting:
   Robert and Peter MacDonald,
   Una Macnamara

AN EQUINOX BOOK

Planned and produced by:
Equinox (Oxford) Limited,
Musterlin House, Jordan Hill Road,
Oxford OX2 8DP, England

Prepared by Lionheart Books

Library of Congress
Cataloging-in-Publication Data
Bailey, Jill
Birds: the plant- and seed-eaters/Jill Bailey
and Steve Parker.
p.   cm. — — (The Encyclopedia of the
   animal world)
Includes index.
Summary: Provides brief descriptions of
birds that eat plants or seeds.

1. Birds – Juvenile literature. 2.
Herbivores – Juvenile literature. 3.
Granivores – Juvenile literature. 4. Birds
– Food – Juvenile literature. [1. Birds. 2
Herbivores. 3. Granivores.]   I. Parker,
Steve. II. Title. III. Series.

QL676.2.B35 1989   598.2'53 - dc19
88-33326 CIP AC

ISBN 0-8160-1964-9

Published in North America by
Facts On File, Inc.,
460 Park Avenue South,
New York, N.Y. 10016

Origination by Alpha Reprographics Ltd,
Perivale, Middx, England

Printed in Italy.

10 9 8 7 6 5 4 3 2 1

FACT PANEL: Key to symbols denoting general features of animals

SYMBOLS WITH NO WORDS

Activity time

● Nocturnal

● Daytime

◐ Dawn/Dusk

○ All the time

Group size

◪ Solitary

◪ Pairs

◪ Small groups (up to 10)

■ Flocks

◪ Variable

Conservation status

☠ All species threatened

⚐ Some species threatened

No species threatened (no symbol)

SYMBOLS NEXT TO HEADINGS

Habitat

◰ General

◣ Mountain/Moorland

◣ Desert

▨ Sea

▨ Amphibious

◿ Tundra

◿ Forest/Woodland

● Grassland

⊗ Freshwater

Diet

■ Other animals

■ Plants

◪ Animals and Plants

Breeding

◎ Seasonal (at fixed times)

◕ Non-seasonal (at any time)

CONTENTS

INTRODUCTION............................5

OSTRICH....................................6
RHEAS 8
EMU 10
CASSOWARIES 12
KIWIS 14
PHEASANTS AND QUAILS.............16
GROUSE 22
GUINEA FOWL AND TURKEYS 26
BUSTARDS 28
PIGEONS 30
SANDGROUSE 32
PARROTS AND PARAKEETS 34
COCKATOOS...............................38
MACAWS 40
HUMMINGBIRDS 42
HORNBILLS 46
TOUCANS 48

MANAKINS 52
COTINGAS 54
BULBULS....................................56
WAXWINGS.................................58
BUNTINGS AND TANAGERS 60
AMERICAN BLACKBIRDS.............66
FINCHES 68
WAXBILLS 72
WEAVERS 74
STARLINGS.................................78
BOWERBIRDS 80
BIRDS OF PARADISE 82
CROWS.......................................86

GLOSSARY 90
INDEX...92
FURTHER READING.....................96
ACKNOWLEDGMENTS.................96

PREFACE

The National Wildlife Federation

For the wildlife of the world, 1936 was a very big year. That's when the National Wildlife Federation formed to help conserve the millions of species of animals and plants that call Earth their home. In trying to do such an important job, the Federation has grown to be the largest conservation group of its kind.

Today, plants and animals face more dangers than ever before. As the human population grows and takes over more and more land, the wild places of the world disappear. As people produce more and more chemicals and cars and other products to make life better for themselves, the environment often becomes worse for wildlife.

But there is some good news. Many animals are better off today than when the National Wildlife Federation began. Alligators, wild turkeys, deer, wood ducks, and others are thriving – thanks to the hard work of everyone who cares about wildlife.

The Federation's number one job has always been education. We teach kids the wonders of nature through *Your Big Backyard* and *Ranger Rick* magazines and our annual National Wildlife Week celebration. We teach grown-ups the importance of a clean environment through *National Wildlife* and *International Wildlife* magazines. And we help teachers teach about wildlife with our environmental education activity series called *Naturescope*.

The National Wildlife Federation is nearly five million people, all working as one. We all know that by helping wildlife, we are also helping ourselves. Together we have helped pass laws that have cleaned up our air and water, protected endangered species, and left grand old forests standing tall.

You can help too. Every time you plant a bush that becomes a home to a butterfly, every time you help clean a lake or river of trash, every time you walk instead of asking for a ride in a car – you are part of the wildlife team.

You are also doing your part by learning all you can about the wildlife of the world. That's why the National Wildlife Federation is happy to help bring you this Encyclopedia. We hope you enjoy it.

Jay D. Hair, President
National Wildlife Federation

INTRODUCTION

The Encyclopedia of the Animal World surveys the main groups and species of animals alive today. Written by a team of specialists, it includes the most current information and the newest ideas on animal behavior and survival. The Encyclopedia looks at how the shape and form of an animal reflect its life-style – the ways in which a creature's size, color, feeding methods and defenses have all evolved in relationship to a particular diet, climate and habitat. Discussed also are the ways in which human activities often disrupt natural ecosystems and threaten the survival of many species.

In this Encyclopedia the animals are grouped on the basis of their body structure and their evolution from common ancestors. Thus, there are single volumes or groups of volumes on mammals, birds, reptiles and amphibians, fish, insects and so on. Within these major categories, the animals are grouped according to their feeding habits or general life-styles. Because there is so much information on the animals in two of these major categories, there are four volumes devoted to mammals (The Small Plant-Eaters; The Hunters; The Large Plant-Eaters; Primates, Insect-Eaters and Baleen Whales) and three to birds (The Waterbirds; The Aerial Hunters; The Plant- and Seed-Eaters).

This volume, Birds – The Plant- and Seed-Eaters, includes entries on rheas, kiwis, pheasants, guinea fowl, pigeons, parrots, hummingbirds, waxwings, finches, starlings and crows. Most of these birds are herbivores; plant material forms the major part of their diet. Together they number over 3,000 species. Within this category are several distinct groups of birds. First, there are the flightless birds such as the ostrich, the emu and the rheas that scientists refer to as the ratites. Second, the game birds – the turkeys, guinea fowl, grouse, pheasants and quails – which include the domestic fowl, man's most useful bird, and the peacocks, with their beautiful feathers used to make fashionable hats. Third, there are many species of perching bird, the passerines, among them the finches, waxbills, weavers, sparrows, starlings and buntings.

The herbivorous birds include several species with unusual diets and/or unique behavior. Many hummingbirds, for example, eat only nectar. They have especially long, curved bills that allow them to probe deep into flowers to take up nectar. Weavers are master architects of the bird world, constructing beautiful domed nests suspended from branches.

Parrots, cockatoos and macaws include many species that are able to mimic sounds, including the voices of people. Finally, there are the starlings, which, with a diet of most fruit, seeds, nectar and pollen, are a major pest of crops, and also have a habit of roosting in cities in flocks of many thousands.

Each article in this Encyclopedia is devoted to an individual species or group of closely related species. The text starts with a short scene-setting story that highlights one or more of the animal's unique features. It then continues with details of the most interesting aspects of the animal's physical features and abilities, diet and feeding behavior, and general life-style. It also covers conservation and the animal's relationships with people.

A fact panel provides easy reference to the main features of distribution (natural, not introductions to other areas by humans), habitat, diet, size, color and breeding. (An explanation of the color-coded symbols is given on page 2 of the book.) The panel also includes a list of the common and scientific (Latin) names of species mentioned in the main text and photo captions. For species illustrated in major artwork panels but not described elsewhere, the names are given in the caption accompanying the artwork. In such illustrations, all animals are shown to scale; actual dimensions may be found in the text. To help the reader appreciate the size of the animals, in the upper right part of the page at the beginning of an article are scale drawings comparing the size of the species with that of a human being (or of a human foot).

Many species of animal are threatened with extinction as a result of human activities. In this Encyclopedia the following terms are used to show the status of a species as defined by the International Union for the Conservation of Nature and Natural Resources:

Endangered – in danger of extinction unless their habitat is no longer destroyed and they are not hunted by people.

Vulnerable – likely to become endangered in the near future.

Rare – exist in small numbers but neither endangered nor vulnerable at present.

A glossary provides definitions of technical terms used in the book. A common name and scientific (Latin) name index provide easy access to text and illustrations.

OSTRICH

An elegant, swan-like brown neck curves above the waving grasses, and a pair of large dark eyes surveys the distant scene. More ostriches stop feeding and raise their heads, their eyelashes fluttering in the dust-laden wind. They pick up the scent of danger. With a few leaps they are off, bounding across the plains with a swaying gait, their wings spread to give them extra lift.

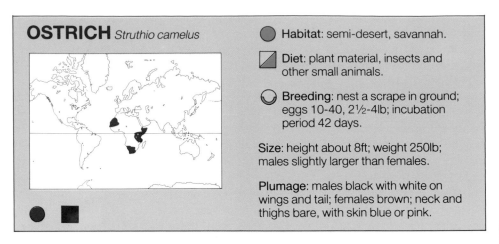

OSTRICH *Struthio camelus*

● Habitat: semi-desert, savannah.

◨ Diet: plant material, insects and other small animals.

◖ Breeding: nest a scrape in ground; eggs 10-40, 2½-4lb; incubation period 42 days.

Size: height about 8ft; weight 250lb; males slightly larger than females.

Plumage: males black with white on wings and tail; females brown; neck and thighs bare, with skin blue or pink.

The ostrich is the world's largest living bird. A large male may be 8ft high and can weigh 300lb. Ostriches cannot fly. Their wings are small relative to their size, but their legs are long and powerful. They have long flexible necks and rather small heads with large eyes. Their heads and necks are almost bare, except for some thin fluffy down and a few bristly feathers. The females have pinkish-gray necks,

▼ A male ostrich stands guard over his eggs and newly-hatched chicks.

the males pink or blue. The legs are also covered in bare pinkish skin.

RECORD-BREAKING RUNNER
The ostrich's body is adapted for running. A fit male ostrich can run at 30mph and keep up that speed for at least half an hour. His top speed is around 45mph. Each stride lifts the ostrich 11½ft into the air.

Ostriches and other flightless birds such as rheas, emus, cassowaries and kiwis have poorly developed flight muscles, and their skeletons lack the large breastbone which is typical of flying birds. These flightless birds are often grouped together and called ratites. Their wing feathers are soft plumes lacking barbs and barbules. This gives ratites a shaggy appearance.

HOOF-LIKE WEAPONS
The ostrich's thigh muscles are large and powerful. It has only two toes on each foot, one much larger than the other. These toes have fleshy pads and act like the hoofs of horses, providing a small surface area to reduce friction with the ground as the bird runs. The leg bones are solid, without the air chambers found in the bones of other groups of birds.

The powerful legs are used for defense on the rare occasions when the bird cannot outrun its enemies or when it is guarding its chicks. A kick from an ostrich can knock over a man.

STRETCH-A-NECK
Ostriches are omnivores – they will eat almost anything. Their main food is shoots, leaves, flowers and seeds, supplemented by small animals such as insects and lizards. They swallow grit and stones to help break down tough seeds and plant material.

Ostriches feed quickly, pecking at one item after another. They collect a lot of food in their mouth, then form it into a ball (bolus) and swallow it. You can see the bolus passing down the ostrich's neck as a large bulge. Ostriches are attracted to very shiny things and will swallow watches and other metal objects.

FARMED FOR FEATHERS
Ostrich feathers have long been used by Africans and Europeans for decorating clothing. In many parts of South Africa ostriches have been farmed for their plumes for over a century. In some places the eggshells are even believed to have magical properties; the shells are also used to carry water. Ostriches are easily domesticated and trained, but do not make good pets – they are too bad-tempered. The main threat to their survival comes from loss of habitat.

COURTSHIP AND PARENTHOOD
Ostriches are polygamous: each male mates with several females. He defends a territory during the breeding

season by displaying aggressively to intruders and by a deep booming call accompanied by inflation of the brightly colored neck skin.

Ostrich courtship is a very showy affair. The male displays to the hen, flapping first one wing, then the other, showing off his white wing plumes. He throws himself to the ground and beats a hollow in the sand with his wings, as if making a nest scrape. Then he lowers his head and waves his wings, uttering little noises. The hen parades in front of him, lowering her head and quivering her wings.

Male ostriches make good parents. The male makes the nest scrape, and the hen may lay up to 12 eggs on alternate days. As many as six or more other females may also lay in the nest, until it contains up to 60 eggs. The male shares incubation duty with the dominant hen: the male, relatively conspicuous, sits on the nest at night, the camouflaged female by day.

The ostrich egg is the largest in the world, up to 6in long and 5in wide. Yet it is only a fraction of the size of the adult bird, so one ostrich can sit on a lot of eggs.

The young chicks are camouflaged in speckled brown coats. If danger threatens, they lie flat on the ground, their necks stretched out, pretending to be dead. They can run around and feed by themselves as soon as they hatch. Their parents stay with them to guard them from birds of prey, hyenas and other predators. When the family are feeding with heads down among the grasses, each parent keeps looking up to scan the area for signs of danger.

▲A male ostrich shows the powerful thighs and tough foot pads typical of the long-distance runner.

►With its huge wings, long neck and legs and great flexibility, the ostrich has a wide range of displays. Here a hen attacks with wings full-spread (1), a hen shows a male she is interested in mating (2), a hen pretends to be injured to lure predators away from her chicks (3), and a cock struts about in a threatening posture (4).

RHEAS

On the Argentinian pampas, large brown birds watch as a male Common rhea displays to attract a mate. With his wings arched high over his body he runs to and fro, swinging his long neck from side to side, uttering a deep-throated call, "nan-doo, nan-doo."

Rheas are large ostrich-like flightless birds up to 5ft tall, with long legs, long necks and soft shaggy brown or gray plumage. Despite their similar appearance, rheas are not related to ostriches. They are more slender, less heavy birds and have three toes instead of the ostrich's two. They are mainly vegetarian, grazing on grass and leaves, but they will also eat insects and a number of other small animals, including lizards.

RHEAS UNDER THREAT

Rheas are in danger of becoming extinct. They have few natural enemies, but are commonly hunted in their native South America. Rheas and their eggs are eaten by local people and their dogs. On agricultural land

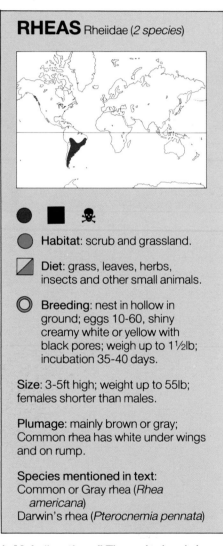

RHEAS Rheiidae (*2 species*)

● ■ ☠

● **Habitat:** scrub and grassland.

◨ **Diet:** grass, leaves, herbs, insects and other small animals.

◎ **Breeding:** nest in hollow in ground; eggs 10-60, shiny creamy white or yellow with black pores; weigh up to 1½lb; incubation 35-40 days.

Size: 3-5ft high; weight up to 55lb; females shorter than males.

Plumage: mainly brown or gray; Common rhea has white under wings and on rump.

Species mentioned in text:
Common or Gray rhea (*Rhea americana*)
Darwin's rhea (*Pterocnemia pennata*)

▶**Male "mothers"** The male rhea brings up the family. Each male collects a harem of 2 to 12 females by his courtship displays (**1**). After mating, the females lay their eggs in the nest the male has prepared (**2**). The male incubates the eggs while the females look for new mates. Once the chicks have hatched, the male leads them to food (**3**).

▲ Common or Gray rheas graze the pampas. Unlike ostriches, rheas have feathers on their neck and legs.

▶ Safe with father. A male Darwin's rhea sits proudly in his nest scrape beside a newly laid egg.

▼ A male Darwin's rhea takes up a threatening posture, with head lowered and wings fluffed up. The white flecks in his plumage distinguish him from the Common rhea.

they are persecuted because they eat crops. Today, rheas exist mainly in remote areas well away from people or in reserves.

EGG COLLECTING

Unlike ostriches, rheas do not need to migrate in search of food. In winter they live in large flocks. But in spring the females gather in small groups, and the males start to fight with one another for dominance, using their necks, beaks and powerful kicks.

Each dominant male rounds up a group (harem) of females. After he has mated with each female, he prepares a nest scrape in the ground, surrounded by a rim of twigs and leaves, then an outer ring of bare ground, which protects the nest from bush fires. The females line up to lay their eggs.

Each female rhea lays one egg every other day for up to 10 days. The male sits on the eggs, and the females return at midday each day to lay more eggs. He may accumulate from 10-60 eggs. The male remains with the chicks for up to 5 months.

A QUICK GETAWAY

Adult rheas rely on speed to escape from danger. If disturbed, they will run away at great speed, often with one wing raised in the air. This seems to help them balance and may act like a rudder in their amazingly rapid twists and turns.

A favorite tactic of an escaping rhea is to double back on its tracks, then fling itself to the ground and "freeze," relying on its camouflage to conceal it in the long grass.

EMU

In the shimmering heat of the Australian outback, a group of long-legged fluffy emu chicks leads their patient father in search of food. Their striped plumage blends with the drying grasses as they peck hopefully at every small object on the ground. Should another emu approach too close, the father is quick to threaten, his golden eyes glowering fiercely under his cap of woolly black feathers.

EMU (*Dromaius novaehollandiae*)

woodland, heathland, desert shrubland and sandy plains.

Diet: plant material, insects and other small animals.

Breeding: nest of twigs or leaves on ground in cover; eggs 9-12, dark green, becoming black with age; incubation period 56 days.

Size: height 5¾ft, weight 110lb; females larger and heavier than males.

Plumage: dark after molting, fading to brown.

Habitat: eucalyptus forest,

The emu is the second largest living bird, standing some 6ft tall. Like the cassowary, it has very shaggy hair-like feathers. Each feather has two shafts of almost equal length that hang limply from the skin. The tail feathers are longer and more widely spaced, so they look rather like a mop. The neck and cheeks are often bare of feathers.

The legs are featherless. The emu has three broad flattened toes and can run at speeds of up to 32mph. It is also a powerful swimmer.

NOMADS

Emus feed on only the most nutritious parts of plants. To find such food in

▶ Doting dad – an emu father stands guard over his eggs and newly hatched chick. He will look after his young family for up to 7 months, attacking any other animals – including other emus – that get too close.

▼ On the move, a large group of emus traveling in search of fresh pastures. They would follow the rains into the cereal-growing farmland were it not for the barrier fence built to keep them out. Up to 70,000 emus may be on the move as the seasons change.

their arid home, they must sometimes travel hundreds of miles each year, following the new growth of plants after the seasonal rains. Emus can put on large amounts of fat – in bad times they may use up over half their body weight of fat.

THE EMU WAR

When farmers deep in the Australian interior opened up new watering places, the emus were able to move into areas which had previously been too dry. But in years of scarce rainfall they were forced to migrate into farmland, where they devoured the crops. In 1932 a company of the Royal Australian Artillery was sent to dispose of the emus. However, the birds' camouflage and avoidance tactics are so good that two machine-guns and 10,000 shells succeeded in killing only 12, and the army withdrew. Farmers continued to shoot them, encouraged by the government. Now a barrier fence 625 miles long has been built to protect the farms.

FASTING FATHER

Emus usually breed in winter, when they form pairs and defend territories of about 12sq miles. The female utters drumming calls to attract the male. Then the two birds lower their heads and sway them from side to side before mating. The hen lays up to 20 eggs in a nest of twigs or leaves situated close to cover. Then she moves off and may take a new mate.

Only rarely does a female stay to guard the male while he sits on the eggs. Usually he is left alone to bring up the family, incubating the eggs and guarding the chicks. While he incubates, he does not eat or drink – he never leaves the eggs unattended.

▶ Emus foraging for seeds in Australian scrubland. Although hidden by the bird's bushy feathers, the wings can be held out, in hot weather, to expose the featherless "under arm" and help the bird lose heat.

CASSOWARIES

In a remote corner of the Northern Australian rain forest, a fierce battle is in progress. With the tearing of branches and thumping of feet, two Southern cassowaries smash their way through the undergrowth in a furious chase. Then they turn to face each other and engage in a savage duel, leaping into the air as they lash out with their sharp spurs.

Cassowaries are rather mysterious jungle birds. They lead solitary lives in the dense tropical forests of Australasia and are seldom seen, so very little is known of their habits. They are large birds with long powerful legs and glossy black plumage. In both sexes, the neck is adorned with brightly colored bare skin and small, fleshy, often bright red flaps called wattles.

PUSHY BIRDS

On the cassowary's head is a huge horny casque up to 6in high. It is thought that the casque may be used to push through the undergrowth. Captive birds use it to turn over soil in search of food. Cassowaries' feathers consist only of drooping quills, so that they appear to be covered in hair rather than feathers. Such feathers do not easily catch in the dense undergrowth. The wing quills are large and spike-like, giving extra protection.

Cassowaries are very bad-tempered birds and have been known to kill humans. Their main weapons are their feet. Each foot has three toes

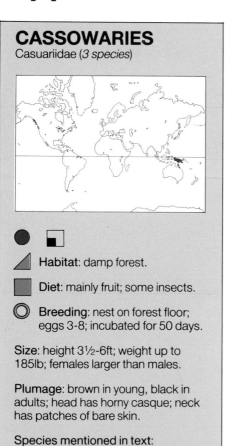

CASSOWARIES
Casuariidae (*3 species*)

Habitat: damp forest.

Diet: mainly fruit; some insects.

Breeding: nest on forest floor; eggs 3-8; incubated for 50 days.

Size: height 3½-6ft; weight up to 185lb; females larger than males.

Plumage: brown in young, black in adults; head has horny casque; neck has patches of bare skin.

Species mentioned in text:
One-wattled cassowary (*Casuarius unappendiculatus*)
Southern or Double-wattled cassowary (*C. casuarius*)

1

2

►Cassowaries are powerful birds, capable of charging at 19mph. Their dagger-like claws make formidable weapons (1). Their coarse hair-like feathers prevent damage by dense undergrowth (2).

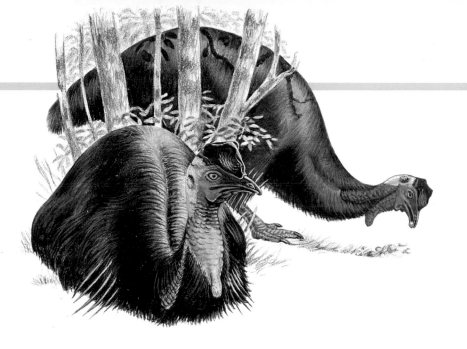

◀A One-wattled cassowary rests while another feeds on fallen fruits. Feeding on fruits and small animals on the forest floor, cassowaries do not need to fly. They have several different color patterns on their necks and wattles.

▼The peculiar appearance of a Southern cassowary. The origin and use of these birds' casque, wattles and "feathers" remain largely a mystery. No-one knows precisely why they have such a strange combination of colors.

armed with long claws, with a dagger-like spike on the inner toe, strong enough to split open a person's body.

FIERCE FATHERS

Cassowaries feed mainly on fruit and need large areas of forest to sustain them. The Southern cassowary eats the fruits of at least 75 tree species – it needs many different species in order to find fruits all the year round. Cassowaries are falling in numbers as the tropical forests are felled or burned. In the breeding season they form pairs and defend territories.

The male approaches the female with a low "boo-boo-boo" call, swelling up his throat and shaking it to show off his brightly colored skin and wattles. As is usual in most ratites (see page 6), the male takes on the duties of caring for the eggs and young. He incubates the eggs in a nest on the forest floor and stays with his chicks for up to a year.

FRIEND OF THE FAMILY?

All three species of cassowary are kept in captivity by the New Guineans, who use their plumes in head-dresses, their quills as nose ornaments and their flesh as food. Cassowaries are also traded for other goods and even for wives. Children play with tame cassowaries, but as the birds grow older they become bad-tempered and vicious and have to be kept in pens.

KIWIS

A shrill "kee-wee" penetrates the moist night air. It is answered by the hoarse "kurr kurr" of a female kiwi. As the repetitive calls come closer, a curious snuffling sound can be heard. A pair of kiwis waddle into the moonlight, scratching at the ground and digging their long curved bills into the soil. Like strange prehistoric animals, they seem to be neither bird nor mammal. Their coats look thick and hairy, yet their large spreading feet are covered in scales.

▼ A Brown kiwi at its nest (1). It rarely lays more than two eggs. The North Island kiwi, a subspecies of the Brown kiwi, drinking (2). Like most birds, kiwis cannot suck – they have to throw back their heads to let the water trickle down their throats.

1

2

KIWIS Apterygidae (3 species)

● ◨ 🐾

◢ **Habitat:** forest and scrub.

◩ **Diet:** insect larvae, worms, spiders, beetles and other small invertebrates.

◎ **Breeding:** nest in holes or burrows; eggs 1 or 2, white, 10-16 ounces; incubation period 65-85 days.

Size: height 10-14in; weight 2½-5lb; females larger and heavier than males.

Plumage: streaked light and dark brown or gray.

Species mentioned in text: Brown kiwi (*Apteryx australis*)

Kiwis are small flightless birds which evolved in the absence of ground-dwelling mammal predators. A kiwi is about the size of a chicken and has no tail. Its tiny wings are completely buried in its feathers. The feathers have no hooked, interlocking filaments (barbules) and look more like coarse hairs. The wing feathers consist solely of quills. Kiwis have three toes, the fourth being represented by a small spur at the back of the foot.

FITTING THE BILL

The kiwi feeds mainly at night. Unlike most other birds, it uses smell rather than sight to find its food and to detect the presence of other birds. Its nostrils open right at the tip of its long curved bill, where they can take in air to smell. At the base of the bill are a series of long, stiff hair-like feathers, much like the whiskers of mammals, which are probably used for touch.

The kiwi feeds very much like a snipe, pushing its bill into the ground and leaving behind small pits as it probes for worms, insect larvae, and other invertebrate prey. On farmland kiwis are useful because they eat many types of crop pests. Kiwis also eat fallen berries and fruits.

GIANT EGGS

Kiwis lay their eggs in holes under tree roots or in burrows, lining them with twigs, grass and feathers. Kiwi courtship is not very spectacular and seems to consist of a lot of chasing, grunting and snorting. They lack any bright colors to display.

The female kiwi is larger than the male and she lays an enormous egg – 14 per cent of her total body weight. It weighs 1lb and measures 5in by 3½in. The egg contains a lot of yolk. The yolk sac remains attached to the newly hatched chick until the chick has consumed all the yolk.

As in most ratites (see page 6), the male incubates the eggs. The newly hatched chicks are already fully feathered – they do not pass through a fluffy down-covered stage. After about a week, the young emerge from the nest and attempt to feed themselves. Kiwis are slow breeders. They lay only one or two eggs at a time, and the young do not breed until they are 5 or 6 years old.

▶ The kiwi is the national emblem of New Zealand. To the native Maori people, it provides a source of food and of feathers for highly valued cloaks.

PHEASANTS AND QUAILS

In the depths of the jungle, a large gray-brown bird is clearing a dance floor of vegetation. His long central tail feathers trail on the ground behind the sheaf of broad wing feathers that are decorated with a row of eye-like spots. This is a male Crested argus. He summons the females with a long plaintive call. As they approach he starts to dance, raising his wings until they meet to form a ruff of feathers around his head, hiding his body. Above this circle wave the long tail feathers. As the feathers catch the Sun, the spots appear to become pearly balls real enough to touch.

The pheasant family includes a wide range of birds, from the tiny Chinese painted quail to the Crested argus, which has the longest tail feathers of any bird in the world. Most are rather heavy birds with plump bodies, short stout legs and rounded wings.

Pheasants and their relatives feed mainly on the ground, scratching to find seeds and fallen fruit, or turning over leaf litter in search of insects. They have strong beaks for dealing with hard seeds, and a large elastic crop, an extension of the gut used to store food. They also swallow small stones to help grind the food. Most pheasants use their feet to scratch for food, but some species, such as the Himalayan monal pheasant, have a shovel-shaped beak with which they dig in soil for roots, bulbs and tubers. Although they prefer to run away from danger, pheasants are mostly strong flyers, but they cannot fly far.

COLORFUL BUT SHY
The birds usually called pheasants are large and colorful with long tails, mostly living in the forests of Asia.

PHEASANTS AND QUAILS Phasianidae
(*183 species*)

Size: length 5½-48in (excluding trains of display feathers); weight 1⅓ ounces-11lb; in some species, males larger than females, sometimes with spurs on their feet.

Plumage: usually brown, gray and heavily marked; males often boldly patterned with blue, black, red, yellow, white or iridescent colors; some species have combs and wattles.

Species mentioned in text:
Blood pheasant (*Ithaginis cruentus*)
Chinese painted quail (*Excalfactoria chinensis*)
Common pheasant (*Phasianus colchicus*)
Crested argus (*Rheinardia ocellata*)
Golden pheasant (*Chrysolophus pictus*)
Himalayan monal pheasant (*Lophophorus impejanus*)
Mountain quail (*Oreortyx picta*)
Peacock (*Pavo cristatus*)
Red jungle fowl (*Gallus gallus*)
Red-legged partridge (*Alectoris rufa*)
Snowcocks (genus *Tetraogallus*)

Habitat: almost every land habitat; varies with species.

Diet: chiefly seeds and fruits; also invertebrates and roots; chicks mostly eat insects.

Breeding: nest a scrape on the ground; eggs 2-20, whitish to olive, sometimes with markings; 16-28 days incubation; period in nest a few hours to several days.

Many have brilliant plumage. There is often a brightly colored patch of bare skin around the eyes. They are shy birds, seldom seen by humans. They creep around the forest floor, communicating with each other by loud raucous calls. At night they roost in trees, out of reach of predators.

Most spectacular are the peacocks, with their spiky crests and (in the males) long trains of feathers. Many peacocks have striking patterns of false eyes on their feathers.

The jungle fowl are the ancestors of our domestic fowl. Their faces are almost bare, and they have fleshy wattles and combs. In the male, the iridescent tail feathers curve up.

Outside the breeding season, most pheasants and peacocks live alone or in family groups. There is little advantage in forming flocks in dense forest.

GRASSLAND SPECIES
Partridges and francolins are stocky birds with short tails. Most species live in open grassland, scrub and semi-deserts. An adaptation to their more open habitat, partridges have dull camouflage colors.

Quails resemble partridges but their wings are long and pointed. Some species can fly long distances and a few migrate hundreds of miles each year with the seasons. Many species have bold black, white, buff or gray markings.

The partridges and quails are more sociable than the pheasants. Their basic unit is a small family group, the covey. In open country coveys often merge into large flocks to feed. Many partridge species have flourished in areas where agriculture has increased the supply of seeds and tubers.

DRESSED FOR DISPLAY

In most pheasants, peacocks and jungle fowl, males are much more brightly colored than females. This plumage is used to attract females during the breeding season. After mating, the males play no further role in bringing up the family. The females, which have to incubate the eggs and guard the young, are dull birds, well camouflaged to protect themselves and their offspring.

▶**Species of pheasant and quail**
Mountain quail (1). Lady Amherst's pheasant (*Chrysolophus amherstiae*) (2). Chukar (*Alectoris chukar*) (3). Common quail (*Coturnix coturnix*) (4). Bobwhite quail (*Colinus virginiatus*) (5).

Many pheasants have iridescent feathers which appear to change in color when viewed from different angles. These colors are produced when light strikes microscopic ridges on the feathers. The duller colors are due to pigments. So astonishingly gaudy are the colors of species such as the Golden pheasant, which lives in rain forests in South-east Asia, that for a long time European naturalists dismissed these birds as figments of the imagination of Chinese artists.

In addition to wing or tail feathers that can be erected into ruffs and fans, pheasants and fowls also have patches of highly colored bare skin around the eyes. Some species also have flaps of skin that dangle at the side of the neck and can be inflated when the bird is excited. Some can also erect crests of feathers on their heads.

The smaller partridges, quails and francolins tend to be more subdued in coloring, and the male and female do not differ strikingly. These birds usually remain faithful to one mate, and both parents help to care for the young.

FIGHTING AND COURTSHIP

Most male pheasants and some quails and partridges defend a territory during the breeding season. This is an area of land containing suitable display grounds and enough food for the male and his harem. He proclaims his territory in a whirring flight. He will fight off any intruder, using the spurs on his legs.

Pheasant displays involve the males adopting positions which show off their plumage. The display may be performed on a special patch within the male's territory that has been cleared of leaves. A courtship call or whistle attracts the females. Ritual feeding movements are important in some species. The peacock female appears to take little notice of her mate as she pecks at the ground, but this is a signal to him that she is very

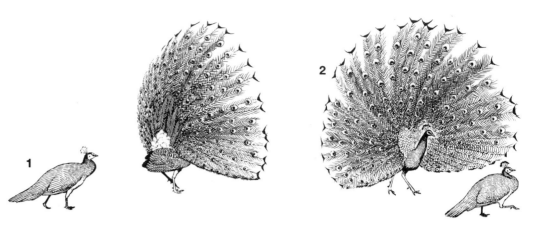

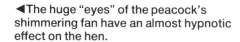

3

4

◄During courtship, the male peacock backs towards the female (1), then turns suddenly (2), exposing her to a shivering constellation of eyes. If interested, she may peck at the ground as if looking for food. Sometimes, just as the male swivels towards the female, he suddenly leaps forwards with a choked hooting sound and tries to grab her. The female usually dashes out of the way (3). But sometimes she hesitates or crouches, and he mates with her (4).

◄The huge "eyes" of the peacock's shimmering fan have an almost hypnotic effect on the hen.

▼Male Golden pheasants of the forests of central China fight over territory, striking out with their spurs.

interested in his advances. The male Common pheasant offers his mate some food before mating.

Most male pheasants and peacocks, as well as some partridges, take several mates in a season. Some, such as peacocks and jungle fowl, stay to guard their harem until the eggs hatch. Others, like the Crested argus, wander off after mating to find new mates.

AT HOME ON THE GROUND
The nests of pheasants and quails are usually simple scrapes in the ground. Only the female incubates the eggs – except that the female Red-legged partridge lays two clutches of eggs, one for the male to incubate and one for herself.

The newly hatched young are well covered in down and can run around soon after hatching. While they are growing, they feed on insects rather than on seeds. They are at great risk for the first month until their wings are developed enough for them to fly into trees to roost at night. Their parents defend them fiercely. Quail cocks have even been known to attack dogs when their mates are sitting at the nest. When on the move, the chicks often stay out of sight under their mother's tail.

WALKING AND HIDING
Many members of the pheasant family prefer to walk rather than fly. The Mountain quails of California may travel up to 40 miles, walking in single file. The snowcocks and Blood pheasants of the Himalayas also march to their feeding grounds in single file.

Pheasants and partridges often hide from danger by keeping very still in cover, then erupting from the ground with a harsh cry and a loud clapping of wings. This alarms and confuses the predator. Many species of open country rely on camouflage and keeping still ("freezing") to avoid detection.

In dense forest, loud warning cries are useful. The cry of the peacock often warns other animals of the presence of leopards and tigers.

GAME BIRDS
Pheasants, partridges, quails and fowls are popular dishes. Some species are plentiful and are hunted legally. Others are overhunted or are suffering the loss of their habitat through felling of the trees or overgrazing; the use of pesticides eliminates the insects on which the young feed.

Several species of these birds have been domesticated. The Red jungle fowl became our familiar farmyard chicken, and partridges and pheasants are reared in many parts of the world as game. Peacocks have been kept as ornamental birds for over 4,000 years around the world.

▼The iridescent plumage of the male Himalayan monal pheasant contrasts with the female's camouflage markings.

▶Hundreds of "eyes" suddenly flash into sight at the climax of the courtship dance of a male Crested argus.

GROUSE

From the distant sagebrush a strange deep-throated popping sound can be heard. On a flat, grassy area a group of Sage grouse cocks are parading importantly, their tail feathers raised in a spiky fan, their neck and breast feathers inflated into a huge quivering ruff. The booming sound comes from a pair of yellow air sacs at the side of the neck which swell and deflate with each pop. The cocks pivot and turn as they show off to the dull sage hens.

▼Two male Black grouse display to each other at a lek to decide who has the right to mate with the female sitting a little way behind.

▼Courtship displays A male Prairie chicken (1) dips its wings, inflates its orange air sacs like balloons and spreads its ruff and tail fan. The male capercaillie (2) erects a very large tail fan and fluffs up the feathers on its neck.

GROUSE Tetraonidae
(*16 species*)

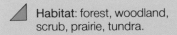

● ■ 🦕

◢ **Habitat:** forest, woodland, scrub, prairie, tundra.

■ **Diet:** adults eat leaves, buds, twigs, flowers, fruits and seeds; chicks eat mainly invertebrates.

◎ **Breeding:** nest a simple scrape in the ground; eggs 5-12, whitish to light brown, darkly blotched; 21-27 days incubation.

Size: length 12½-36in; weight ⅔-14lb; in some species males much larger than females.

Plumage: males black or brown, with white markings, and combs red to yellow; females brown and black flecked with white; ptarmigan white in winter.

Species mentioned in text:
Black grouse (*Lyrurus tetrix*)
Blue grouse (*Dendragapus obscurus*)
Capercaillie (*Tetrao urogallus*)
Hazel grouse (*Bonasa bonasia*)
Prairie chicken (*Tympanuchus cupido*)
Red grouse (*Lagopus lagopus scoticus*)
Ruffed grouse (*Bonasa umbellus*)
Sage grouse (*Centrocercus urophasianus*)
Spruce grouse (*Dendragapus canadensis*)
White-tailed ptarmigan (*Lagopus leucurus*)

◄Burrowing into snow, White-tailed ptarmigan lie low to stay out of chilling winds and avoid predators.

Grouse are plump, stocky birds. They have short stubby bills and feed on the ground, mainly on plant material and some insects. Their short wings provide for powerful bursts of flight over short distances. When disturbed, they often glide low over the ground, but they prefer to run to the nearest cover. Most grouse have dull, camouflage colors, but even in these species striking colors and markings may be revealed during courtship displays. Many grouse have colorful patches of bare skin above the eyes which can be inflated during displays.

PREPARED FOR WINTER

Grouse live in temperate and cold climates. They have dense plumage, with feathers covering their nostrils and legs. In winter, ptarmigan grow feathers on their toes which act like snowshoes. Other grouse species develop projecting horny plates on each toe which serve the same purpose. These are shed in spring.

Ptarmigan also grow much longer claws in winter to help them dig in the snow for food and shelter. In the tundra and high mountains, ptarmigan molt to white camouflage plumage in winter.

Grouse can cope with the food shortages of winter. They have very large food stores in their guts. Bacteria in the gut help them make the most of poor quality food. They can also eat conifer needles, which other animals find either poisonous or distasteful. In winter, grouse may remain quiet and still for hours, using up little energy or food. They are a valuable source of food for northern predators such as foxes and birds of prey.

◄White-tailed ptarmigan hens molt to a summer plumage that blends with the surrounding moorland.

COMMUNAL DISPLAYS

Many species of grouse perform communal courtship displays at traditional sites called leks. Within the lek, each cock holds his own small territory. The central territories are especially desirable, as they will attract the most hens. Before the hens arrive, the cocks display and fight to establish a ranking order which determines who gets which territory.

These displays can be spectacular. Many cock grouse are able to erect the feathers on their necks like a ruff. Their tail can be fanned out, often revealing striking markings and white undertail feathers. Inflatable air sacs of brightly colored bare skin are common. These make a booming sound when inflated and deflated.

Some species, such as the capercaillie and Spruce and Blue grouse, display alone in their territories. The Ruffed grouse from North America "drums," thumping the air with his vibrating wings.

LIVING WITH MOTHER

After mating, the hen leaves the lek to lay her eggs alone. The nest is a leaf-lined scrape in the ground. The young can run around soon after hatching, but need to be guarded and kept warm under their mother's feathers at night for a week or two. She feeds them insects until they can find food for themselves. In species such as the Hazel grouse, permanent pairs are formed, and the cock guards the hen while she incubates the eggs.

GROUSE IN DANGER

Grouse are a popular dish. The Red grouse and Ruffed grouse are reared for sport in many parts of the world. However, the survival of many species is seriously threatened by loss of habitat to forestry and agriculture.

▶ The courtship display of the cock Sage grouse is one of the most spectacular seen – and heard – among birds.

In the hot scrubland of central Australia, a Mallee fowl waits patiently at the foot of a large mound of sand, watching her mate dig down to the egg chamber below. Slowly, his powerful feet remove some 72 cubic feet of sand. Then she inspects the chamber to select a suitable site for the next egg. After she has laid it, the cock returns to begin the task of rebuilding the mound.

Guinea fowl and turkeys are sturdy birds with strong legs, often armed with spurs in the males. They have stout beaks, capable of dealing with small vertebrates such as frogs and lizards, as well as seeds and nuts. They are ground feeders, scratching at the ground with their claws. Although they can fly quite strongly for short distances, they prefer to walk or run. Turkeys are essentially forest birds, but many species of guinea fowl live in open steppes and grassland.

MOUND-BUILDING
The megapodes include the Brush turkey, Common scrub fowl and Mallee fowl. They are famous for using the heat given off by rotting vegetation to incubate their eggs. They pile moist leaf litter into a mound, or place it in a pit with a mound of soil or sand over it to prevent it blowing away. The birds regulate the temperature of the mound by adding or removing soil or sand according to the relative temperatures of the mound and the surrounding air. Scrub fowl mounds are the largest structures made by birds – up to 16½ft high and 40ft in diameter.

GRUMPY GOBBLERS
The Common turkey lives in small, single-sex flocks, which split up during the breeding season. Within these flocks, the males fight for dominance,

GUINEA FOWL AND TURKEYS Numididae, Meleagrididae, Megapodiidae (20 species)

 Habitat: varies; woodland, rain forest or grassland, depending on species.

Diet: seeds, fruits, roots, bulbs, tubers, invertebrates and small vertebrates.

Breeding: guinea fowl and turkeys nest in scrapes in the ground; megapodes build heaps of rotting vegetation; eggs: guinea fowl 4-12, turkeys 8-15, megapodes 5-33; 23-28 days incubation.

Size: length: guinea fowl 15-22in, turkeys 36-48in, megapodes 11-24in; weight: guinea fowl 2½-3½lb, turkeys 6½-20lb, megapodes 2-17½lb; turkey males may be twice weight of females.

Plumage: turkeys generally dark, with metallic reflections of bronze and green; guinea fowl black, often spotted with white; megapodes brown or black.

Species mentioned in text:
Brush turkey (*Alectura lathami*)
Common scrub fowl (*Megapodius freycinet*)
Common turkey (*Meleagris gallopavo*)
Crested guinea fowl (*Guttera pucherani*)
Mallee fowl (*Leipoa ocellata*)

▶▼**Building a compost heap** The strange nest-mounds of the megapodes are unique among birds. The male Mallee fowl works on the nest throughout the year, digging a pit, filling it with moist leaf litter and covering it with sand (**1a**). He leaves a central chamber in which the female will lay her eggs (**1b**). The heat from the decaying plant material (**1c**) incubates the eggs. The male Brush turkey uses his feet to pile up rotting vegetation (**2**).

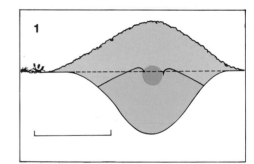

sometimes killing each other with their slashing spurs. During the breeding season, courtship takes place at special "strutting grounds" where the males display to the females. The most dominant males get to mate most. The females are left to incubate the eggs and rear the young by themselves.

BALD BUT BRIGHT
The heads and necks of guinea fowl and turkeys are covered in brightly colored bare skin. Fleshy flaps of skin, called wattles, dangle from their chins and necks. These inflate during displays. The birds like company, and the bright colors may act as signals to keep the flock together. Guinea fowl often have large crests or horny casques on their heads too.

GROUP ACTION
Guinea fowl live in large flocks. In the early morning, the dominant males lead the flocks to water, all marching in single file. Later they will line up abreast of each other to sweep the area for food. As soon as one bird finds food, the others rush up and jostle for position to steal it.

◀The elegant Crested guinea fowl has white bead patterning on black plumage and a head-dress of curly black feathers.

▼Already larger than its mate, the male Common turkey appears twice its size when it fans its tail and fluffs its feathers.

BUSTARDS

A male Great bustard is trying to impress a female. His tail is raised and fanned, his wings held back and twisted so that the secondary feathers form huge white rosettes on either side of the body. The neck is inflated like a balloon, the mustache feathers forming a stiff spiky frame to his face. The female is unmoved – she has seen it all before.

Bustards are large secretive birds of the open plains. They spend most of their lives on the ground, seldom taking flight. With their long sturdy legs and long necks, they look rather like small ostriches. Their feet have only three forward-pointing toes; they do not need a hind toe because they do not perch in trees.

The name bustard means slow bird. Bustards hunt insects and small vertebrates by stalking slowly through the grassland with head held high. They are all strong flyers, but prefer to hide or run to escape danger. The houbara can reach speeds of 25mph when running. Bustards also use their wings and bill to defend themselves and may turn round and squirt sticky droppings at an enemy.

BUSTARDS IN RETREAT

Many bustard populations are now threatened with extinction because their grassland is disappearing fast due to cultivation.

Some species, such as the houbara and the Nubian bustard, are hunted, especially in the Middle East and

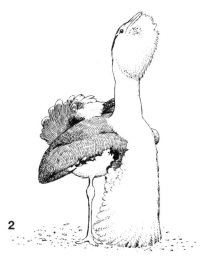

▲**Male courtship displays** The houbara (1) raises its white neck-ruff over its head. The Australian bustard (*Ardeotis australis*) (2) inflates the neck into a long drooping sack. The Great bustard (3) inflates its neck like a balloon and erects the feathers of its tail and wings.

◄Most bustard species are African. This Black korhaan male is from Namibia.

central Asia. There, bustards are a popular prey for falconers.

SHY BIRDS

Bustards are very seldom seen. Their coloring camouflages them against their dry grassland habitat, but striking patterns on the wings show up in flight. If frightened, bustards often crouch close to the ground, becoming almost invisible.

Baby bustards can run around soon after they hatch. Their mottled down blends with the colors of the ground. Only the female incubates the eggs, but the male usually helps to guard the chicks. When danger threatens, the parents cry a faint warning, and the chicks run for shelter. They can fly after 5 weeks, but usually stay close to their mother for several months.

►Female Little bustard. Loss of grasslands has reduced this species' range in Europe to Spain, Portugal and part of southern France.

▼The Kori bustard is widespread in Africa and is one of the largest of all flying birds, weighing up to 40lb.

PIGEONS

The soft cooing on the white-stained window-ledge stops. With a loud clap of wings, the pigeons flutter down to the street below. There, on a bench sits an old lady surrounded by excited pigeons, feeding from her hand, perching on her shoulders and waddling along the pavement, their heads jerking with eagerness as they search for the scraps of bread.

Many pigeons thrive in contact with humans. Descendants of one species, the Rock dove, have become the familiar Feral pigeons of our streets, nesting on buildings instead of cliff ledges. Another species, the Collared dove, has spread rapidly over Europe, taking advantage of urban gardens.

Pigeons are plump birds with compact bodies, short legs and a small head and bill. The larger species are usually called "pigeons," the smaller species "doves." At the base of the bill is a fleshy area of bare skin. Most species are rather drab and very well camouflaged. A few, especially the fruit doves, are brightly colored.

Pigeons feed on a variety of plant material and also on snails, worms and insect larvae. Many species, such as the Wood pigeon, have a large crop, an extension of the gut used to store food. Unlike most other birds, pigeons suck up water instead of throwing back their heads and letting it trickle down their throats.

COOING COURTSHIP

Male pigeons try to attract a female by a bowing display. The male lowers his head and leans forward, puffing out his neck and cooing gently. Some doves raise and fan out their tails as

▲The Spotted dove from the Far East feeds on the ground on a wide variety of seeds and berries. It fills its crop with seeds, then retreats to a safe place to digest its meal.

▼A flurry of white doves outside a mosque in Afghanistan. These birds are descended from white breeds of the Rock dove.

PIGEONS Columbidae
(*about 300 species*)

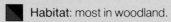

Habitat: most in woodland.

Diet: mainly fresh green leaves and buds, fruits or seeds.

Breeding: usually a twig nest in trees; eggs usually 1 or 2; many species have several broods; 13-35 days incubation; nestling period 14-35 days.

Size: length 6-33in; weight 1 ounce-5¼lb.

Plumage: mostly dull gray or brown.

Species mentioned in text:
Collared dove (*Streptopelia decaocto*)
Passenger pigeon (*Ectopistes migratorius*)
Rock dove or Feral pigeon (*Columba livia*)
Spotted dove (*Streptopelia chinensis*)
Turtle dove (*S. turtur*)
Victoria crowned pigeon (*Goura victoria*)
Wood pigeon (*Columba palumbus*)

well. Once a potential mate shows interest, he may preen and feed her – she will stick her beak inside his, just like a young pigeon.

The newly hatched young (squabs) are fed on pigeon "milk" by both parents. The "milk" is produced in the parent bird's crop. Much like a creamy cheese, it contains protein, fat, minerals and vitamins. The parent bird regurgitates the "milk," and the young thrust their heads into their parents' beaks to feed on it. As the young grow, the parents mix the milk with partly digested food.

FAST FLYERS

Pigeons are fast, strong flyers. Racing pigeons can reach speeds of 45mph. Their wing muscles make up over a third of their body weight. Many pigeons, such as the Turtle dove, migrate many thousands of miles to the south in winter, returning north to breed in summer. For thousands of years pigeons have been used to carry messages. The Romans used them, and so did soldiers in the Second World War. A carrier pigeon can travel 630 miles in a day.

CITY BIRDS

While pigeons may be a tourist attraction, they can also be a nuisance, soiling buildings and stealing grain.

Even though some pigeons occur in huge numbers, they are relatively slow breeders, and shooting can have a devastating effect. The Passenger pigeon of North America nested in colonies several square miles in area. By the end of the 18th century there were probably about 3,000 million Passenger pigeons. By 1914 they were extinct, due mainly to overhunting. Today, several species of pigeon are endangered by the destruction of their woodland habitat.

▶Young Turtle doves beg regurgitated food and pigeon milk from their parent. They leave the nest when 2 weeks old.

▼The largest pigeon of all, a male Victoria crowned pigeon of New Guinea raises his crest in a bowing display to woo his mate.

SANDGROUSE

As the Sun rises over the Negev desert, the Spotted sandgrouse fly in to drink at a small pool, wheeling and turning as they descend. Soon the pool is ringed with birds, jostling for the best places. Thirsty after the long night, the sandgrouse drink quickly, without lifting their heads.

Sandgrouse are pigeon-like birds with short legs and long pointed wings which enable them to fly fast to get away from predators. They live in dry grasslands and deserts, spending most of their lives on the ground. Their soft gray, brown or buff plumage camouflages them well; and with their short legs and crouching posture they cast little give-away shadow. The males are more brightly colored than the females, often having a contrasting breast band. Unlike pigeons, sandgrouse have no patch of bare skin at the base of the bill.

LIFE AT GROUND LEVEL
Sandgrouse roost in hollows on the ground, often in flocks of several hundred, made up of small family groups. Their soft, thick plumage provides warmth during the cold desert night yet also protects them from the heat of the Sun. Feathers covering the base of the bill help to keep the sand out of their nostrils. They have spreading toes to help them walk on soft sand.

SPEEDY SEED-EATERS
Sandgrouse feed mainly on seeds, pecking frequently at the ground and walking quite fast as they feed. They store the seeds in their crop, an extension of the gut, and digest them later in a safer place. Seeds have hard shells, and the sandgrouse often swallow grit to help grind them down. The crop can hold around 9,000 seeds.

Like pigeons, sandgrouse are able to suck up water. When drinking, they dip their bills in the water and close their nostrils with little flaps.

FLYING WATER CARRIERS
Seeds contain very little water, so sandgrouse have to drink frequently. They will often fly 10 or 20 miles to favorite watering holes every morning and evening. The flocks converge as they approach the water, forming huge gatherings of thousands of birds.

▲ The female Pin-tailed sandgrouse, from south-western Europe and Central Asia, is very well camouflaged in her scrubland surroundings.

► Namaqua sandgrouse fly in to drink at a waterhole in south-western Africa. The males soak their breast feathers with water to take back to their chicks.

Young sandgrouse cannot fly. Even when big enough to leave the nest, it may be several months before they are strong enough to fly long distances to water. Instead, their father brings the water to them in a most unusual way – absorbed in his belly feathers. First he rubs his belly in the sand to remove the waterproofing oil with which the feathers are coated. Then he wades into the water up to his belly, keeping his head and wings out of the water. He kneels down and rocks to and fro to let the water soak into his belly feathers, which act like a sponge. Even after flying back to the nest, there is still plenty of water for the chicks to suck. The female can also carry water in this way. However, her feathers are not so absorbent.

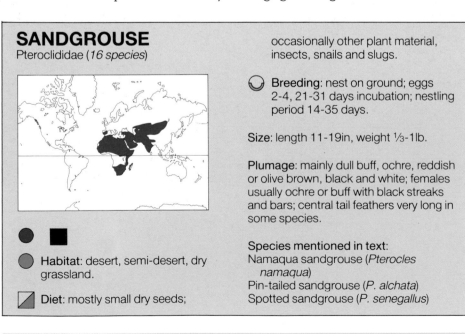

SANDGROUSE
Pteroclididae (16 species)

Habitat: desert, semi-desert, dry grassland.

Diet: mostly small dry seeds; occasionally other plant material, insects, snails and slugs.

Breeding: nest on ground; eggs 2-4, 21-31 days incubation; nestling period 14-35 days.

Size: length 11-19in, weight ⅓-1lb.

Plumage: mainly dull buff, ochre, reddish or olive brown, black and white; females usually ochre or buff with black streaks and bars; central tail feathers very long in some species.

Species mentioned in text:
Namaqua sandgrouse (Pterocles namaqua)
Pin-tailed sandgrouse (P. alchata)
Spotted sandgrouse (P. senegallus)

PARROTS AND PARAKEETS

As the African savannah starts to shimmer in the heat of the midday Sun, a flock of Fischer's lovebirds bursts out of the long grass, their bright green wings flashing in the sunlight. Chattering noisily, they settle out in pairs among the thorny branches of a favorite acacia tree to roost. Male and female nuzzle together, touching bills and preening each other as if they have just been reunited after a long parting.

Parrots are found in most parts of the tropics and subtropics. The Austral conure lives as far south as Tierra del Fuego, and the Carolina parakeet, which became extinct in 1914, once occurred as far north as New York State. Parrots are very sociable birds and usually go around in pairs or flocks. Most species live in wooded areas, but a few live in open grassland or glades, using occasional clumps of trees for shelter.

The large head, short neck and hooked bill easily distinguish parrots from other birds. Many parrots are brilliantly colored, often with contrasting patches on the head, wings or tail. Some parrots have a patch of bare-colored skin around the eyes, which makes the eyes look larger than they really are. Their bright colors and their ability to imitate the human voice when kept in captivity have made parrots popular caged birds for thousands of years.

RIGHT- OR LEFT-FOOTED

The feet of parrots have a powerful grip. The two outer toes point backwards, the two inner ones forwards, so the toes act like pincers for grasping branches and food. Parrots are the only birds which hold their food in one foot while they eat. Parrots may be either right- or left-footed. They are pigeon-toed and waddle as they walk.

PARROTS AND PARAKEETS Psittacidae
(part only: *293 species*)

Habitat: mainly lowland tropical and subtropical woodland.

Diet: mainly plants: fruits, nuts, seeds, buds, nectar and pollen; sometimes small insects.

Breeding: usually nest in holes in trees, more rarely in burrows or termite mounds; a few species build communal nests; 1-8 small eggs. 17-30 days incubation; nestling period 21-90 days.

Size: length 4-24in.

Plumage: varies; brilliant green, red, yellow, blue, white and black; many species have long tail feathers.

Species mentioned in text:
African gray parrot (*Psittacus erithacus*)
Amazons (*Amazona* species)
Austral conure (*Enicognathus ferrugineus*)
Australian king parrot (*Alisterus scapularis*)
Budgerigar (*Melopsittacus undulatus*)
Carolina parakeet (*Conuropsis carolinensis*)
Fischer's lovebird (*Agapornis fischeri*)
Golden-shouldered parrot (*Psephotus chrysopterygius*)
Great-billed parrot (*Tanygnathus megalorhynchus*)
Green-rumped parrotlet (*Forpus passerinus*)
Ground parrot (*Pezoporus wallicus*)
Kakapo (*Strigops habroptilus*)
Kea (*Nestor notabilis*)
Monk parakeet (*Myihopsitta monachus*)
Patagonian conure (*Cyanoliseus patagonus*)
Rainbow lorikeet (*Trichoglossus haematodus*)
Scaly-breasted lorikeet (*T. chlorolepidotus*)

A THIRD FOOT?

Parrots have a large, down-curving, hooked upper bill which overlaps the smaller upward-curving lower bill. The narrow pointed tip of the bill is used for delicate tasks such as preening and, in some species, extracting insects from cracks in the bark. The powerful beaks of some parrots can break open nuts which a person could not open by hitting with a rock.

The upper bill is attached to the skull by a special kind of hinge, which enables it to be used as a kind of grappling hook for climbing. In fact, parrots often use their bill like an extra foot when clambering around the tree-tops. The underside of the upper bill often has a series of ridges that act as a file, to keep the edges of the lower bill sharp. In species such as the Great-billed parrot of Indonesia,

▼Lorikeets all in a row. The bird at the top is a Scaly-breasted lorikeet; the rest are Rainbow lorikeets.

▲A budgerigar leaves it nest-hole in a tree in the Australian outback. Most wild budgerigars are green.

▼This male Australian king parrot is 16in long and lives in dense woodland. Its bill has a waxy sheen.

which has an unusually large and conspicuous bright red bill, the bill may also be used for displaying to others in its flocks.

FLOWER POWER

Most parrots are vegetarians. The strong beak is needed for crushing the hard shells of nuts and seeds, and the hook is used to tear open fruit. The lories and lorikeets feed in a different way. They lap up nectar from flowers using their brush-tipped tongue.

Most parrots feed in the tree-tops, but some smaller species, especially the parakeets, parrotlets, budgerigars and lovebirds, feed on grass seeds on the ground. Some can become pests when they steal grain from farmland.

Because different plants produce flowers and fruits at different times of year, some parrots will fly long distances in search of food. Rainbow lorikeets, which rely on flowers, will fly 50 miles between neighboring Pacific islands.

TALKING PARROTS

Parrots are famous for their ability to imitate the human voice. The most skilled mimics are the African gray parrot and the amazons. In the wild, they make many different sounds – chatters, squeaks, shrieks, clicks and screams – but do not appear to mimic the calls of other species.

No-one knows why parrots "talk" in captivity. But because they are very sociable birds, in captivity they may be mimicking humans to try to communicate with them since there are no other parrots around. Where several birds are kept together, they do not "speak" much.

Parrots are inquisitive birds. One gray parrot called Alex was able to

name 23 different objects, 5 colors, and 4 shapes, count numbers up to 5 and respond to several commands.

HOME-MAKERS

Most parrots nest in holes in trees, often high above the ground. They line the nest hole with wood dust or sometimes with grass and leaves. Some species, such as the Australian Golden-shouldered parrot, establish their holes in termite mounds. The presence of the termites may help to keep predators away from the nest.

A few species, for example the Patagonian conure and the Australian Ground parrot, live in burrows. Some lovebird species steal the ready-made nests of weaverbirds. South American Monk parakeets build huge nests of twigs high in the tree-tops, in which each pair has its own chamber.

COURTSHIP AND PARENTHOOD

Most parrots pair for life. They stay together all year round and often feed and preen each other. To attract his mate, the male displays in front of her – bowing, hopping, flicking his wings, wagging his tail feathers and strutting to and fro. Some parrots expand the brightly colored irises of their eyes when they are excited. This is called eye-blazing.

The New Zealand kakapo is the world's only flightless nocturnal parrot. Like his cousin the kea, the male kakapo mates with several different females. The males meet at night and advertise themselves with very loud booming calls. Females visit them and select their mates.

Both parrot parents help to rear the young. The male feeds the female while she sits on the eggs, then helps to collect food for the young. Newly hatched parrots are blind and helpless, needing to stay with their parents for several weeks or even months. The parents regurgitate food to feed the young. The larger parrot species may live for 50 years or more.

PARROTS LARGE AND SMALL

There are several distinctive groups of parrot. The keas are large birds with long narrow beaks. They live above the New Zealand treeline and scavenge like crows. The lorikeets and lories are nectar-feeders with brush-tipped tongues. Parakeets are small parrots with long pointed tails, while lovebirds have short, rounded tails. Pygmy parrots are the smallest parrots. They creep around tree trunks in the same way as small woodpeckers, hunting for insects.

PARROTS IN DANGER

Their brilliant plumage and popularity as pets have been the downfall of many parrot species. Over-collecting for the pet trade and for their feathers has caused the extinction of many species. Others have declined because of the destruction of their forest habitat. Over two dozen species of parrot have become extinct in the last 200 years, and many more are endangered today.

◀**Representative species of parrot** Rainbow lorikeet (1). Fischer's lovebird (2). Female Eclectus parrot (*Eclectus roratus*) (3). Black-capped lory (*Lorius lory*) (4) showing tongue adapted for lapping up nectar. Crimson rosella (*Platycercus elegans*) (5). Red-capped parrot (*Purpureicephalus spurius*) (6). Blue-crowned hanging parrot (*Loriculus galgulus*) (7). Tiny hanging parrots roost upside down like bats. Kea (8).

▶A pair of Green-rumped parrotlets from South America. Despite their reputation for gaudy coloring, most parrots are mainly green.

COCKATOOS

From the crown of a pandanus palm comes a grating sound, and the patter of shells falling on the ground below. A Great black cockatoo is attacking a palm nut clasped in its left foot. Patiently it saws away with its sharp beak until it can get the hooked point of its bill into the hole to slice at the kernel. Then its spoon-shaped tongue takes up the pieces.

Cockatoos are colorful parrots with a crest of feathers on their heads that they can raise or lower at will. They have square tails and quite rounded wings. Although they are sometimes kept as pets, they are not very good talkers in captivity. The name "cockatoo" comes from the Malayan word *cacatua*, meaning "pincers," a reference to the cockatoo's toes. The two outer toes of each foot point backwards and grip in the opposite way to the two forward-pointing inner toes.

SAFETY IN NUMBERS
Like many parrots, most cockatoos travel around in large noisy flocks. This way there are many pairs of eyes

1

2

COCKATOOS Psittacidae
(part only: *17 species*)

● ■

▲ Habitat: woodland or open country with clumps of trees.

■ Diet: seeds, nuts and insects; a few species eat bulbs and roots.

◎ Breeding: nest in holes in trees; 2-4 small dull white eggs; 20-30 days incubation; nestling period 60-70 days.

Size: length 13-32in.

Plumage: usually white, pink or black, often tinged with yellow.

Species mentioned in text:
Galah cockatoo (*Cacatua roseicapilla*)
Gang-gang cockatoo (*Callocephalon fimbriatum*)
Great black or Palm cockatoo (*Probosciger aterrimus*)
Slender-billed cockatoo (*Cacatua tenuirostris*)
White-tailed cockatoo (*Calyptorhynchus baudinii*)
Yellow-tailed cockatoo (*C. funereus*)

to look out for danger. Also, the cockatoos often post a sentry on a suitable look-out perch high in a tree.

Cockatoos' main enemies are large birds of prey, but monitor lizards and large snakes can climb trees to steal eggs, young and even sitting adults. A group of squawking cockatoos will put off many predators. At best only one bird at a time can be caught, so it is safer in the crowd.

SHOW-OFFS

The cockatoos' crest is used for displaying to other birds. The male bird courting a female will draw attention to his raised crest by bobbing and swinging his head. In some species,

such as the Gang-gang cockatoo, the male's crest is a different, brighter color than the female's. If angry or threatened, a cockatoo will raise its crest, so it looks considerably bigger than it really is.

SKILFUL BILLS

Cockatoos eat many different kinds of food. Their powerful sharp-edged bills enable them to break open tough nuts and seeds, and some cockatoos swallow sand to help grind up the shells in their stomach. Cockatoos often add insects to their diet when there are not many seeds around.

Several species, such as the White-tailed and Yellow-tailed cockatoos, peel off the bark of eucalyptus trees and bore holes in the trunk to get at insect larvae. A few cockatoos dig for the underground parts of plants, such as roots and bulbs. The Slender-billed cockatoo has a bill with a long point that it uses like a digging-stick.

NOISY PESTS

Cockatoos that live in semi-desert areas, where food is found only in scattered patches, often form huge flocks numbering over 1,000 birds. These roam long distances in search of food. Seed-eaters like the Galah cockatoo can become great pests in grain fields. They have even invaded towns and cities where, being rather careless birds, they are frequently run over by cars. Because Galahs are such noisy birds when in a crowd, Australians often use the word "galah" to describe a stupid person who cannot stop talking.

◄Representative species of cockatoo
Sulphur-crested cockatoo (*Cacatua galerita*) (1). Yellow-tailed cockatoo (2). Rose cockatoo (*C. moluccensis*) (3). Great black or Palm cockatoo (4). Such large cockatoos are highly conspicuous and most have prominent upward-pointing crests on their heads. Males and females are either very similiar or identical in appearance.

MACAWS

With loud shrieks that penetrate deep into the South American jungle, a small group of Scarlet macaws bursts out of the tree-tops. As they fly across the clearing, their brilliant colors glow in the sunlight. A noisy crowd is gathering on a cliff of salty clay to lick minerals.

The macaws are the largest of the parrots. They have long tapering tails and powerful wings for flying over the forest canopy. They have brilliant-colored plumage in which several colors often blend together. Some macaws have striking markings round the eyes. In most species, there is a large patch of pale bare skin around each eye. When the bird is excited, its cheeks blush pink.

FOREST FLYERS

Macaws are powerful flyers, and can live in the highest part of the canopy, traveling far in search of fruiting trees. Their beaks are so strong that macaws can hang suspended by them from branches. They can chisel their way into the toughest of nuts. A macaw can file through 1/10in-thick wiring to get out of a cage.

The harsh calls of macaws help them to communicate in dense vegetation. When a male and female are alone together, they use a range of

MACAWS Psittacidae (part only: *about 18 species*)

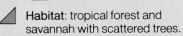

● ◻ ☠

◣ **Habitat:** tropical forest and savannah with scattered trees.

◻ **Diet:** nuts, seeds, fruit.

◎ **Breeding:** nest in holes in trees; 2-4 white eggs; about 28 days incubation; nestling period about 3 months.

Size: length 13-40in.

Plumage: brilliant red, blue, yellow or green.

Species mentioned in text:
Blue-and-yellow macaw
 (*Ara ararauna*)
Green-winged or Red-and-green
 macaw (*A. chloropera*)
Hyacinth macaw (*Anadorhynchus
 hyacinthinus*)
Lear's macaw (*A. leari*)
Scarlet or Red-and-yellow macaw
 (*Ara macao*)

▶A Blue-and-yellow macaw, a large species often kept in captivity, where it breeds very well.

◄The Hyacinth macaw is the largest macaw and a popular pet. Collecting for the pet trade and hunting for food are fast reducing the numbers of almost every species of wild macaw. The Hyacinth macaw lives in a part of the Amazonian rain forest which is rapidly being felled and settled, so its future is very uncertain.

▼In spite of their names, the Green-winged (or Red-and-green) macaw and the Scarlet (or Red-and-yellow) macaw have most of the other seven colors of the rainbow as well.

clicks and quieter sounds. When feeding, macaws are surprisingly silent, the only sound being the patter of nutshells falling to the forest floor below.

Pet macaws once saved the lives of the people in a Caribbean village in Panama. When the invading Spaniards arrived close to the village, the tame macaws got excited and screamed loudly enough to alert the villagers.

BABY FOOD
Young macaws are born naked and helpless, staying with their parents for about 3 months. Like many other baby parrots, they are fed on food regurgitated from the parent's crop.

DANGEROUS SPLENDOR
The splendid macaws seem to symbolize the exuberance of the life of the tropical rain forest. But, like the forest itself, their continued existence is threatened. As the forest is felled, the macaws lose their habitat. Their brilliant plumage and popularity as pets have led to over-hunting and some species have already become extinct. As a species becomes rarer, its value in the pet trade increases. A rare species like Lear's macaw, which is known only from one remote part of Brazil, will fetch up to $20,000 a bird. Macaws are also hunted for food by local people, since they are tasty birds.

HUMMINGBIRDS

The loud whine of a chainsaw shatters the quiet of a Central American forest. Within seconds a tall tree crashes down into flower-laden bushes nearby. A cloud of small, brightly colored birds rises in fright from the bushes. Many hummingbirds have lost their territories and their nectar-laden flowers (and so probably their lives) to the loggers.

A few species of hummingbird live in North America, as far north as Alaska, while others are found in the far south of South America. However, most species of these tiny, dazzlingly-bright birds live in Central America and northern South America, near the Equator.

A century ago they were caught, stuffed and used to decorate the hats of rich and fashionable women. Fortunately, they are no longer at risk from this sad trade. Today, the main threat to many hummingbirds is the destruction of their natural forest, shrubland and grassland homes, and the raising of crops or livestock in these areas. It is thought that about 40 species of hummingbird are now threatened with extinction.

HUMMING TO THE FLOWERS

The main food of all hummingbirds is nectar – the sweet, sticky "honey" made by flowers. As a hummingbird hovers in front of a flower, its wings beat so fast that they produce the humming noise that gives the birds their name. The long, pointed bill is pushed deep into the flower to reach the nectar, and the bird sucks up the nectar with its long, tube-like tongue. Different species of hummingbird have different shaped bills, which are

HUMMINGBIRDS
Trochilidae (*315 species*)

● ▪ ✦

▨ **Habitat:** mainly forest and shrub-land.

▨ **Diet:** nectar, small insects.

○ **Breeding:** 1 clutch in spring or rainy season, possibly a second later; 1 or 2 white eggs per clutch; incubation 14-23 days.

Size: length 2-9in; weight $\frac{1}{15}$-$\frac{2}{3}$ ounce.

Plumage: glittering greens and blues, often with other bright colors on the head and breast; males usually have more brilliant plumage.

Species mentioned in text:
Broad-billed hummingbird (*Cynanthus latirostris*)
Emeralds (genus *Amazilia*)
Hermits (genus *Phaethornis*)
Sicklebills (genus *Eutoxeres*)
Sunbeams (genus *Aglaeactis*)
Sword-billed hummingbird (*Ensifera ensifera*)

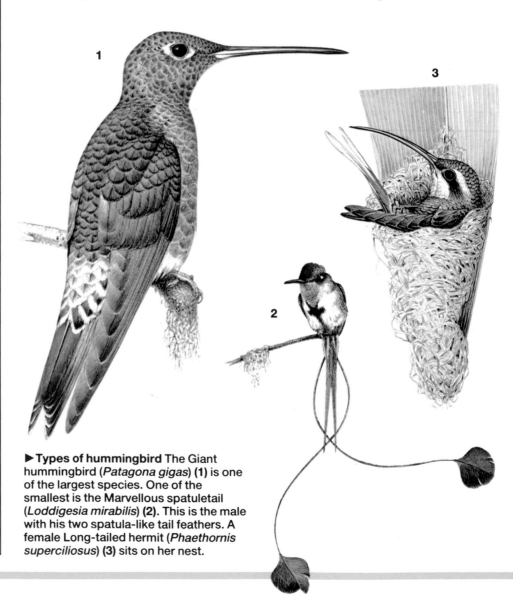

▶ **Types of hummingbird** The Giant hummingbird (*Patagona gigas*) **(1)** is one of the largest species. One of the smallest is the Marvellous spatuletail (*Loddigesia mirabilis*) **(2)**. This is the male with his two spatula-like tail feathers. A female Long-tailed hermit (*Phaethornis superciliosus*) **(3)** sits on her nest.

suited to flowers of a particular shape. The sicklebills, for example, specialize in feeding from heliconia flowers, which are the identical down-curved shape as the birds' bills.

Hummingbirds are so small that they lose body heat quickly so they need to take in plenty of energy. A hummingbird eats more than half its own weight in food each day. Nectar is rich in energy-giving sugars and is an ideal food for these tiny, busy fliers.

Flowers benefit from a hummingbird's visit. As the bird feeds, it collects pollen dust on its bill and face. When it visits another flower, it may leave the pollen there (cross-pollination),

▶Hummingbirds are the only birds that can hover. The wing twists near the body at the "wrist," pushing air downwards on the "down" stroke (1-5), and swiveling to do the same on the "up" stroke (6-10).

▼More hummingbirds Showing their gleaming colors are a Bee hummingbird (*Mellisuga helenae*) (1), Amethyst woodstar (*Calliphlox amethystina*) (2), Frilled coquette (*Lophornis magnifica*) (3), and Ruby-topaz hummingbird (*Chrysolampis mosquitus*) (4). The Sword-billed hummingbird (5). A White-tipped sicklebill (*Eutoxeres aquila*) (6). A Bearded helmetcrest (*Oxypogon guerinii*) (7).

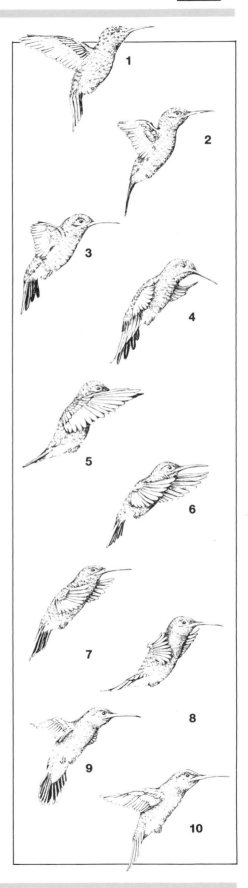

so helping the flowers to produce seeds and therefore to spread.

As well as feeding on nectar, most hummingbirds occasionally eat small insects and other tiny creatures. They catch them on the wing or pick them off leaves and twigs.

MEETING A MATE

In some hummingbird species, such as emeralds and sunbeams, each bird lives in its own territory, which contains enough flowers to provide food. As the patch of flowers dies away, the bird transfers its territory to another area where there are plenty of fresh flowers. In other species, such as the hermits and the Sword-billed hummingbird, each individual regularly visits groups of long-flowering plants that remain in bloom right round the year.

These habits mean that hummingbirds come together only at breeding time. Males from an area collect in one place, called a "lek." Here they sing their simple, squeaky songs and display their vivid plumage to the watching females. After mating, the female builds a nest and raises the young; the male plays no further part.

Most hummingbirds build deep cup-shaped nests from moss and soft plant material. The nests are usually attached to twigs by cobwebs and hidden deep in the vegetation.

When the nestlings hatch out, the mother feeds them while hovering in front of them. She puts her bill into the youngster's mouth and pumps in a regurgitated mash of nectar and insects. After leaving their nest, the fledgling hummingbirds are still fed by their mother for up to 40 days.

▶A Broad-billed hummingbird approaches a flower to take nectar, its wing-beats "frozen" by high-speed photography. Most hummingbirds can beat their wings up to 80 times a second.

HORNBILLS

With a raucous squawk and a loud whooshing of wings, a large and ungainly looking bird flaps across a forest clearing in Sarawak, Malaysia. Its enormous bill is topped by a rhino-like "horn." A group of tourists, at the edge of the clearing, watch the bird through binoculars and click with their cameras. They have seen Sarawak's national emblem, the Rhinoceros hornbill.

The hornbill's large, strong bill is made of a hard, horny substance and is used for a variety of jobs, such as picking fruit or catching small creatures to eat. More puzzling is the "casque" – the bulbous growth on top of the bill.

The casque is not solid horn, but a thin layer of skin and bone enclosing a light, spongy tissue. Only one species, the Helmeted hornbill of South-east Asia, has a solid casque, which is made of a golden, ivory-like substance. Various reasons have been suggested for the casque, such as to help the birds recognize the sex and age of other individuals, to use as a weapon in fights, or to knock fruit from trees.

PRISONER ON THE NEST

In all hornbills except the two African ground-dwelling species, the female becomes a "prisoner" for many weeks as she sits on her nest.

Hornbills nest in holes in trees, rock faces and earth banks. The female partly blocks the entrance to the hole with mud from the outside; she is sometimes helped by the male. Then she enters the nest and continues to block up the entrance from inside, this time using her own droppings and food remains. Again, in some species, the male helps by bringing pellets of sticky mud or food.

Finally only a narrow slit is left, through which the male feeds his partner as she incubates the eggs. When these hatch he must bring food for the chicks too.

▼ **Types of hornbill** The Rhinoceros hornbill (1) is one of the larger species and is named after the rhino-like horn on its casque. The Great hornbill (*Buceros bicornis*) (2) of Asian forests is 4ft in length. The Helmeted hornbill (3) has a solid, ivory-like casque. Von der Decken's hornbill (*Tockus deckeni*) (4).

HORNBILLS Bucerotidae
(*45 species*)

Habitat: forest; some African species live on grassland.

Diet: most species, fruit and/or insects; ground hornbills, small mammals and reptiles.

Breeding: any time of year in forest, rainy season in grassland; 1 or 2 eggs in larger species, 4-7 in smaller species; incubation 25-40 days.

Size: length 15-64in; weight 3 ounces-9lb.

Plumage: mainly black and white, gray and brown; bill and bare skin of face and throat often red or yellow.

Species mentioned in text:
Helmeted hornbill (*Rhinoplax vigil*)
Rhinoceros hornbill (*Buceros rhinoceros*)
Southern ground hornbill (*Bucorvus cafer*)
Yellow-billed hornbill (*Tockus flavirostris*)

▲Southern ground hornbills live in groups and have various displays. This female "bill-fences" under a male's chin (1). She then brings insects as "presents" for the male, to strengthen their partnership (2). The female may also beat her bill on the ground and flash her wing feathers at the male (3).

One male of a South-east Asian species of hornbill made an average of 13 trips each day for 4 months to feed his family, regurgitating about 15 pieces of fruit each time. Meanwhile his partner passed droppings and food remains out of the slit, to keep the nest clean.

In some species, the female breaks out of her nest hole when the chicks are about half grown, so that she can help to feed the young.

THE PICK-AXE BILL

The larger forest hornbills are mainly fruit-eaters and travel widely in search of food. Most of the smaller species eat chiefly insects, with some fruit in season. The very large ground hornbills are carnivores, using their beaks like pick-axes to spear and batter prey such as hares, squirrels, tortoises and the occasional snake.

►This Yellow-billed hornbill, a widespread African species, makes short work of eating a long snake.

TOUCANS

TOUCANS Ramphastidae
(*37 species*)

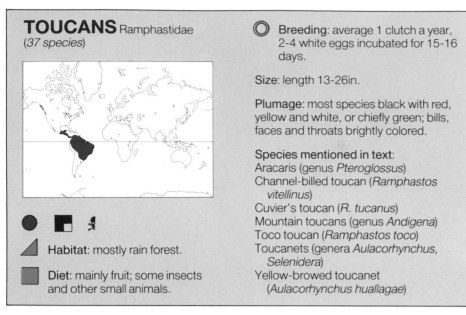

⬤ ■◱ ☠

◺ Habitat: mostly rain forest.

■ Diet: mainly fruit; some insects
and other small animals.

◯ Breeding: average 1 clutch a year,
2-4 white eggs incubated for 15-16
days.

Size: length 13-26in.

Plumage: most species black with red,
yellow and white, or chiefly green; bills,
faces and throats brightly colored.

Species mentioned in text:
Aracaris (genus *Pteroglossus*)
Channel-billed toucan (*Ramphastos
vitellinus*)
Cuvier's toucan (*R. tucanus*)
Mountain toucans (genus *Andigena*)
Toco toucan (*Ramphastos toco*)
Toucanets (genera *Aulacorhynchus,
Selenidera*)
Yellow-browed toucanet
(*Aulacorhynchus huallagae*)

**At dusk in a Brazilian forest,
a group of toucans croak and
hop among the branches.
Their black bodies are almost
invisible, but their yellow-and-
orange bills glow warmly in
the light of the setting Sun.
The birds clack bills together
and toss pieces of fruit, which
they catch in their bill-tips.**

Toucans have long been favorite birds
of artists, photographers and nature-
lovers. The Toco toucan is probably
the best known species. It has a
bright-eyed expression, a huge and
colorful bill with the trace of a smile,
and a white throat patch and black
body feathers like a person's dinner
suit and shirt.

PLAYING "CATCH" WITH FRUIT?
The toucans' behavior is also well
known – and puzzling. They generally
live in straggling groups and when
perching together in a tree they sometimes seem to play. They toss a piece
of fruit to each other, much like our
game of catch. Or two toucans may
clasp bills and then push and "wrestle"
until one gives up – but there are no
signs of aggression, as when fighting
off predators. Whether these activities
are play, simply for the fun of it, or
whether they help to keep the members of a group together, is not clear.
  Toucans live in Central and South
America, except for the cold far south-
west of the continent. The group

◀The Channel-billed toucan is widespread across northern South America.

▶**Types of toucan** An Emerald toucanet
(*Aulacorhynchus prasinus*) **(1)** giving its
call. A Black-billed mountain toucan
(*Andigena nigrirostris*) **(2)** searches for
fruit, a Chestnut-mandibled toucan
(*Ramphastos swainsonii*) **(3)** swallows a
berry, while a Toco toucan **(4)** stretches
to pick food. A Guianan toucanet
(*Selenidera culik*) **(5)** examines a
possible nest hole. A Saffron toucanet
(*Andigena bailloni*) **(6)**. A Collared
aracari (*Pteroglossus torquatus*) **(7)**.

includes toucans themselves, which comprise 10 species in the genus *Ramphastos*. These large birds have mainly blackish plumage and are found in lowland rain forests.

The 11 species of aracaris are all smaller and more slender, and they also live in forested lowlands. The 12 species of the mainly green-colored toucanets vary in size from small to large. Some toucanets live in the cooler Andean rain forests, at heights of about 10,000ft, and rarely descend into the warm lowlands. The four species of little-known mountain toucans dwell even higher. They live in the Andes Mountains, from northwest Venezuela to Bolivia.

BERRY-PICKING BILL
All toucans are mainly fruit-eaters, picking food with the bill-tip and tossing it upwards and back into the mouth to be swallowed.

Although the bill looks heavy, it is in fact very light. It is made of a horny outer sheath covering a hollow "box," which is strengthened by slim, criss-crossing rods of bone. The toucan, being a large and weighty bird, has to perch on thicker branches. Yet its bill gives it a long reach, so that it can stretch out to pick berries and other fruits from the thin and delicate outermost twigs of trees.

The Toco toucan has the largest bill of any toucan; it may be almost one-third of the bird's total length of about 26in.

WEAPON OR "PERSONAL FLAG"?
Being able to reach out for food may explain the length of the bill, but why is it so thick and brightly colored? Over the centuries naturalists have suggested many reasons. It may be a conspicuous weapon that frightens smaller birds, so that the toucan can raid their nests and steal their eggs and young. Or it might be a form of identity, a sort of "personal flag." Each individual has a slightly different size, color and pattern of bill. This would allow each bird to recognize others in its group, others of its species (which is particularly important when looking for a mate) and also toucans of other species with which it may compete for food or living space.

TREE-TOP TOUCANS
Toucans spend most of their lives high in the tree-tops. They feed there, bathe there in pools of rainwater that collect in hollow branches, use their long bills to preen each other – and breed there, in holes in tree trunks.

A suitable nest hole has an entrance just large enough for the toucan to squeeze through, but its depth may vary from only a few inches to 6ft. Most larger toucans utilize a natural cavity usually resulting from the decay of tree trunks. Some smaller species

◄A Toco toucan delicately holds two berries in its huge, saw-edged bill as its strong feet grip an old tree tunk.

may take over a hole made by a woodpecker, sometimes evicting the owners. The toucan might attempt to enlarge the hole, but its bill is not nearly so strong as the woodpecker's bill, and it usually has little success. A suitable nest hole may be used year after year.

WELL-HEELED BABIES

Toucan parents do not line their nest hole. The eggs are laid on a bed of wood chippings and regurgitated seeds. The male and female take it in

▼The toucan's great bill (this is Cuvier's toucan) is used to pluck food from twigs and for preening.

turns to incubate the eggs, but they rarely remain at their task for more than an hour at a time. They often leave the eggs uncovered, and if they are disturbed by intruders, they fly away rather than stay on the nest and use their great bills as weapons. When the eggs hatch, the babies have padded, spike-covered heels that protect them from rubbing against the wood and seeds under their feet.

Newly-hatched baby toucans cannot see and have no feathers. They are fed by both parents and after about 6 to 7 weeks, their feathers grow and they learn to fly. In the aracaris, the parents, each night, lead their young back to the nest hole. Even out of the

breeding season, these toucans sleep in holes. In other species, the young roost among the foliage, with their parents and others in the group.

Young toucans have comparatively small, drab bills. As they grow, their bills grow bigger and take on the bright colors of their parents.

UNDER THREAT

Since toucans generally live in remote forests, many species have not yet been studied in detail in the wild. One species, the Yellow-browed toucanet from Peru, is now threatened, and some species are becoming rarer as their forest homes are cut down for timber and to make way for farmland.

MANAKINS

With sharp, high-pitched calls, a small white-throated bird perches in a clearing deep in the South American forest. Suddenly it begins a series of rapid flights, up and down, twisting and turning to show off its bright patches of color. It is a male White-bearded manakin, hoping to attract a mate. A few yards away another male starts the same courtship display, then another, until the whole area is alive with fluttering males trying to out-dance their rivals.

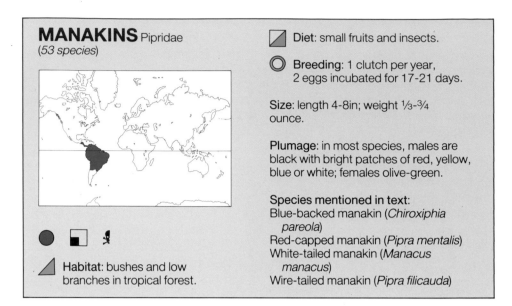

MANAKINS Pipridae
(*53 species*)

⬛◻ 🐾

🔺 Habitat: bushes and low branches in tropical forest.

◨ Diet: small fruits and insects.

○ Breeding: 1 clutch per year, 2 eggs incubated for 17-21 days.

Size: length 4-8in; weight ⅓-¾ ounce.

Plumage: in most species, males are black with bright patches of red, yellow, blue or white; females olive-green.

Species mentioned in text:
Blue-backed manakin (*Chiroxiphia pareola*)
Red-capped manakin (*Pipra mentalis*)
White-tailed manakin (*Manacus manacus*)
Wire-tailed manakin (*Pipra filicauda*)

Manakins are small, active birds of the warm forests in Central and South America. Like many other birds they live in bushes and on low branches, feeding on insects and fruit, which they obtain by rapid dashes from a favorite perch. Also like other birds, they have mainly dark plumage on the body with vivid patches of color on the head, chest and legs.

DANCING DOWN AT THE LEK
Unlike most other birds, however, the manakins have some of the most extraordinary courtship displays in the bird world.

In the breeding season, males of one species come together in a display area called a lek. Each male clears himself a patch of forest floor, moving away twigs and leaves. He then begins an amazing series of rapid display flights, to impress the females. He dashes between perches, swoops and dives, utters short, sharp calls, and

▶**Types of manakin** A Long-tailed manakin (*Chiroxiphia iinearis*) **(1)**. A Cirrhate manakin (*Teleonema filicauda*) **(2)**. A Lance-tailed manakin (*Chiroxiphia lanceolata*) **(3)**. A Golden-headed manakin (*Pipra erythrocephala*) **(4)**. Gould's manakin (*Manacus vitellinus*) **(5)**.

snaps together special wing feathers to make cracking sounds.

The male Wire-tailed manakin goes even further. He backs towards the female and wiggles his rear so that his two long, wire-like tail feathers brush her under the chin.

DUET FOR ONE

In yet other species, such as the Blue-backed manakin, two males sing and dance together to attract a female. Their songs are so similar and well-timed that they sound as if they come from a single bird. But slowed-down tape-recordings show that one male, the dominant one, begins each note about 1/20th of a second before his partner. When the female comes near, the dominant male changes his tune – a signal for the other male to leave.

The amazing "dance of the manakins" is yet one more reason why the tropical forests should be conserved for the future.

ONE-PARENT FAMILY

The males take no part in bringing up the young. The female makes a delicately-woven cup nest, slung from two twigs of a low plant, often near a forest stream. Up to 3 weeks after the eggs are laid, they hatch – this is an unusually long time for such a small bird. The female then feeds her brood on a regurgitated mixture of fruit and a variety of insects.

COTINGAS

A loud, metallic "clang" shakes the warm, still air of a tropical forest. A group of travelers, who have stopped their car to rest, look around in surprise. They decide to explore. After walking for almost a mile through the jungle, following the sound, they eventually discover its source. It is a pale, brown-speckled, thrush-like bird with an enormously wide mouth – a male bellbird, singing his mating call.

COTINGAS Cotingidae
(*65 species*)

 Habitat: forest.

 Diet: fruit and insects.

○ Breeding: usually 1 clutch per year, 1-3 blotched eggs incubated for 19-28 days.

Size: length 3-20in (most species 6-10in); weight 1/5-14 ounces.

Plumage: from dull browns and grays (especially in females) to reds and blues (mainly in males).

Species mentioned in text:
Bellbirds (genus *Procnias*)
Guianan cock-of-the-rock (*Rupicola rupicola*)
Kinglet calyptura (*Calyptura cristata*)
Peruvian cock-of-the-rock (*Rupicola peruviana*)
Umbrellabirds (genus *Cephalopterus*)
White-cheeked cotinga (*Ampelion stresemanni*)

The four species of bellbird belong to the extremely varied cotinga family. The sound made by the male to attract a mate is one of the loudest calls of any bird. When a female comes near, the pair go through a complicated court-ship dance, bobbing and posturing.

A VARIED FAMILY
Cotingas live in Mexico and Central and South America. They inhabit forests – but this is about all they have in common. Within the group are some tiny birds only 3in long, such as the Kinglet calyptura from the mountains of south-eastern Brazil (this species may now be extinct). At the other extreme are the bulky umbrellabirds, which are the size of a large crow.

Plumage also varies, from the pale speckles of the bellbirds to the brilliant blues, purples, reds and whites of males in other species. Diet, too, varies among the cotingas. Some eat mainly insects, while others concentrate on fruits. The White-cheeked cotinga of the Andes Mountains in Peru seems to eat only the berries of two types of mistletoe. It regurgitates the sticky seeds and wipes them from its beak on to a branch, so helping the plants to spread from tree to tree.

NEST STUCK TO A CLIFF
Female cotingas construct the nest, incubate the eggs and feed the chicks.

▲ **Types of cotinga** The calfbird (*Perissocephalus tricolor*) (1) is named after the male's low, mooing call as he displays to the female. The Masked tityra (*Tityra semifasciata*) (2). The Pompadour cotinga (*Xipholena punicea*) (3). The Swallow-tailed cotinga (*Phibalura flavirostris*) (4).

► A pair of Peruvian cock-of-the-rock. The male (on the right) is brighter in color, like most species of cotinga.

Most cotingas construct flimsy nests shaped like cups or saucers among the twigs. In the cock-of-the-rock, however, the female makes a half-cup-shaped nest of mud and small roots, glued together and stuck to a sheer rock face with her own saliva. Since there are few such rocky outcrops in the forest, nest sites are limited and several females may build very close to one another.

Many cotingas, like manakins (see page 52), have elaborate dances by which the male attracts the female before mating. Guianan cock-of-the-rock males gather together at a display area (a lek), where each clears an area or court on the ground. When a female approaches, the males fly down from their perches and crouch on the bare earth with feathers spread and heads on one side to show their crests, each looking at the female with one beady eye.

BULBULS

Young children, playing in a patch of wasteland in an Asian town, lose their ball in thick bushes. As they search for it, one of them spots a bird's nest in the fork of a branch. Inside are four thick-shelled eggs, pale pink and patterned with reddish patches and swirls. The children remember what they have been taught, and leave the nest alone. From a distance, they soon see the owners return – a pair of adult bulbuls.

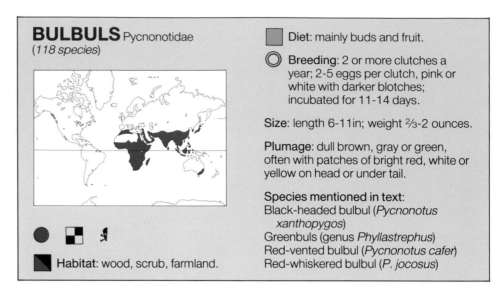

BULBULS Pycnonotidae
(*118 species*)

Diet: mainly buds and fruit.

Breeding: 2 or more clutches a year; 2-5 eggs per clutch, pink or white with darker blotches; incubated for 11-14 days.

Size: length 6-11in; weight ⅔-2 ounces.

Plumage: dull brown, gray or green, often with patches of bright red, white or yellow on head or under tail.

Species mentioned in text:
Black-headed bulbul (*Pycnonotus xanthopygos*)
Greenbuls (genus *Phyllastrephus*)
Red-vented bulbul (*Pycnonotus cafer*)
Red-whiskered bulbul (*P. jocosus*)

Habitat: wood, scrub, farmland.

Bulbuls are smallish, bulky birds with very short wings and slender, down-curved bills. Many species are shy and hide in thick woodland. Others live in open country, and some have spread into farmland and city suburbs, where they come to bird tables in chattering flocks. Many people like their bustling manner and their pleasing, cheerful song. In some areas, bulbuls are kept in cages as songbirds.

Bulbuls build their nests in trees and bushes, usually between 5 and 30ft from the ground. The nests are rarely well hidden, however, so that cats, crows and lizards often find them and steal many of the eggs and chicks. Cuckoos, too, often lay their eggs in bulbul nests.

Male and female bulbuls look similar, although the male is easier to spot at breeding time since he spreads his square-ended tail and flutters his wings to attract a mate. Both parents take turns to incubate the eggs, and both feed their young. Usually a pair has two or more broods each year.

A NOISY PEST
Originally, the various species of bulbul ranged across Africa, the Middle East and India to China and the islands of South-east Asia. However, some species were sent abroad to be kept in cages as songbirds. They managed to escape from captivity and now they live wild in many new places. For example, Red-whiskered bulbuls are found in North America and Australia, while Red-vented bulbuls dwell in Fiji and other tropical Pacific islands.

These introduced birds may look lively and sound cheerful, as they roam in noisy groups around gardens and public parks. However, they have damaged valuable crops, especially fruit. Also they eat food that would otherwise have fed native birds.

At the other end of the scale, nine species of bulbuls are now thought to be very rare and under threat. These include three species of greenbuls from the island of Madagascar, where many other animals are also in danger.

▼ **Types of bulbul** The three species shown here have the distinctive hair-like feathers that form a head crest, typical of many bulbul species. They are the Red-whiskered bulbul (1), the Red-vented bulbul (2), and the Black bulbul (*Hypsipetes madagascariensis*) (3).

►Alert and noisy, bulbuls are usually among the first animals to react to danger, such as a hawk or cat. Here Red-whiskered bulbuls squawk and threaten a snake, which now has no hope of sneaking up and snatching one of them.

▼A Black-headed bulbul of South-east Asia, photographed at its nest.

WAXWINGS

The cutting winter wind sweeps in from the North Sea across eastern England. A flock of brownish birds, with long head crests, bright wings and yellow tail tips, moves slowly along a hedgerow. The birds hungrily eat the berries. In an hour they have gone, leaving the hedge almost bare. They will probably not be back in this area for several years. For it is a "waxwing winter," when thousands of Bohemian waxwings fly to Britain from mainland Europe for the winter months.

WAXWINGS Bombycillidae
(*8 species*)

● ■

△ Habitat: wood and forest.

▨ Diet: fruit and insects.

◎ Breeding: 1 clutch per year, 2-7 eggs incubated for 12-16 days.

Size: length 7-10in.

Plumage: browns, grays and black, with some red and yellow patches.

Species mentioned in text:
Bohemian waxwing (*Bombycilla garrulus*)
Cedar waxwing (*B. cedrorum*)
Gray hypocolius (*Hypocolius ampelinus*)
Japanese waxwing (*B. japonica*)
Phainopepla (*Phainopepla nitens*)
Silky-flycatchers (genera *Phainoptila, Ptilogonys*)

Bohemian waxwings (often simply called waxwings) are regular winter visitors to eastern Britain. Usually they come in small numbers. Every few years, however, large numbers appear here and roam the countryside in search of fruit. They are not shy birds and may come into parks and gardens to search for berries or to feed at a bird table.

These waxwings breed during the summer in the far north, in Arctic and sub-Arctic regions such as Finland. Every few years, however, their numbers increase, and groups spread out from their normal range to more southerly areas. Some of these wanderers turn up in Britain. In earlier times their appearance was thought to mean that bad luck was on the way, and they were called "pest-birds" in some places. What causes the changes in waxwing numbers is not yet clear.

FAST IN FLIGHT
Besides the Bohemian waxwing there are two other species of true waxwings in the family. These are the Cedar waxwing of North America and the Japanese waxwing. They are strongly-built birds with long wings and powerful flight. The speed of the

▲In summer, Cedar waxwings fly north from Mexico and the southern USA to breeding grounds in Canada and the northern USA.

Cedar waxwing on the wing has been measured at 29mph. Although they rely chiefly on fruit for food, they also eat petals and insects in summer, catching such prey as dragonflies.

COURTSHIP PRESENTS
During the winter, waxwing flocks wander in search of food. Gradually they form pairs, a male and female passing an object such as a berry between them several times as part of their courtship. In spring the pair build a loose, bulky nest of twigs, grass and lichens, lined with fine grasses, mosses and pine needles. The nests are built in trees at heights of up to 56ft, well away from the trunk. They often look like piles of twigs that have collected by chance on a branch. The male feeds the female as she sits on the eggs; both partners feed the chicks when they hatch.

THE SILENT WAXWING
A fourth member of the waxwing family is the Gray hypocolius, from

the Tigris-Euphrates Valley in the Middle East. It too is mainly a fruiteater, taking dates, figs and mulberries. Waxwings are generally quiet birds, except in the breeding season or sometimes when feeding. Yet the Gray hypocolius has no known song and spends a considerable part of its time hidden in foliage.

Also in the waxwing family are four species of silky-flycatcher, named for their soft, silky looking plumage. They eat berries, petals and insects, making spectacular flights from high perches to catch several insects in one short trip. The best-known silky-flycatcher is the phainopepla, which lives in desert scrub from the south-west USA to central Mexico.

▲A Bohemian waxwing catches an insect on the wing. The red ends, like wax droplets, on the secondary wing feathers gave these birds their name.

▼The phainopepla's name means shining robes; the male has silky feathers.

BUNTINGS AND TANAGERS

In southern Canada, near the Great Lakes, children go for a walk during their school nature lesson to see a new bird in the area. The rosy red cardinal has been spreading north for many years, helped by seeds put out by people in winter.

Longspurs, tree sparrows, grassquits, flower-piercers, dacnises, euphonias, chlorophonias, grosbeaks, cardinal grosbeaks, cardinals, thrush tanagers, honeycreepers, saltators and finches, as well as the buntings and tanagers themselves, all belong to the huge and enormously varied bunting family.

The main groups are true buntings (Emberizinae, 281 species), tanagers and honeycreepers (Thraupinae, 233 species) and cardinal grosbeaks (Cardinalinae, 37 species). (A different group of honeycreepers, the Hawaiian honeycreepers of the finch family, are shown on page 70.)

TERRITORIES LARGE AND SMALL

More than three-quarters of all the species in the bunting group are found in North, Central and South America. They are mostly dumpy birds with stout, cone-shaped bills adapted for crushing and taking the husks off seeds. In the breeding season, male birds have territories which they defend against other males of their species. The American tree sparrow has a territory of 2½ acres or more, and feeds within the borders of its territory. Other buntings have small territories, perhaps no more than 1,200sq yd in area, so they go elsewhere to feed.

Most bunting species are monogamous (one male pairs with one female). They build neat, compact, cup-like nests from grass and weeds, and use soft material, such as hair, moss and feathers to line their nests. The mother sits on the eggs and

BUNTINGS AND TANAGERS Emberizidae
(553 species)

● ■ ☠

■ Habitat: from Arctic tundra to scrub and tropical forest.

▢ Diet: mainly grains and other seeds; insects; some take nectar.

◯ Breeding: 1-3 clutches per year; 2-6 eggs; incubation 10-18 days.

Size: length 4-11in; weight ⅓-1⅓ ounces.

Plumage: varies from drab browns and grays to brilliant reds and blues.

Species mentioned in text:
American tree sparrow (*Spizella arborea*)
Azure-rumped tanager (*Tangara cabanisi*)
Cardinal (*Cardinalis cardinalis*)
Lapland longspur (*Calcarius lapponicus*)
Plush-capped finch (*Catamblyrhynchus diadema*)
Rainbow bunting (*Passerina leclancherii*)
Red-legged honeycreeper (*Cyanerpes cyaneus*)
Swallow-tanager (*Tersina viridis*)

nestlings, although the father helps to feed the chicks as they grow and learn to fly. Once the breeding season is over, the territories break down and the buntings gather in loose flocks to feed and roost.

TROPICAL TANAGERS

Tanagers are colorful birds of the American tropics. Their main food is fruit, and they digest the fleshy parts but not the seeds – so these birds are probably the most important spreaders of seeds for tropical American trees and shrubs. Honeycreepers belong to this group. They sip nectar from flowers with their long, thin, down-curved bills.

Among the cardinal grosbeaks are familiar birds of parks and gardens in North America and also little-known species in tropical rain forests. One of the most familiar is the cardinal itself, the male with his black throat and warm, red plumage that glows amid the winter snows. Thanks largely to people who put out seeds in winter, this species has spread hundreds of miles northwards in this century, so that now it breeds in several parts of southern Canada.

►▼**Types of bunting and tanager**
A Swallow-tanager (1). A Red-legged honeycreeper (2). A Plush-capped finch (3). A White-throated sparrow (*Zonotrichia albicollis*) (4). A Rose-breasted grosbeak (*Pheucticus ludovicianus*) (5). A Buff-throated saltator (*Saltator maximus*) (6). A Rose-breasted thrush tanager (*Rhodinocichla rosea*)(7). A Corn bunting (*Emberiza calandra*) (8).

▲The Lapland longspur (this one is a male), a type of bunting, is named from its long toes.

▼The male Red-legged honeycreeper has blue breeding plumage, which changes to green for the rest of the year.

ODD-SPECIES-OUT

There are two odd-species-out, given their own groups within the bunting family. One is the Swallow-tanager of northern South America. It breeds at heights above 3,300ft and spends the rest of the year in the warm lowlands. It is a highly social bird and often performs mass displays.

The second species is the Plush-capped finch from western South America. Its appearance is known from a few museum specimens, but it is rarely seen in the wild. It is thought to live along woodland edges and clearings in the cloud forests of the Andes, and feed close to the ground on insects.

IDEAS ON EVOLUTION

The bunting family includes some of the most famous birds in science: 13 species of Galapagos finches, sometimes called "Darwin's finches." They live on the Galapagos Islands, in the eastern Pacific. The famous English naturalist Charles Darwin stopped here in the 1830s, when he was on a five-year voyage round the world on the HMS *Beagle*. He noticed that the finches on the Galapagos Islands all looked very similar, but their bills were different.

►The Rainbow bunting, from Mexico, is one of 60 species of bunting found in North America.

Darwin suggested that long ago, only one species flew to the islands. There it evolved into many different species. The present-day species of Galapagos finches avoid competing with one another by living in different places, such as on the ground or in trees, and by taking different sorts of food. For example, some feed on large seeds, while others eat small seeds, or insects on leaves and twigs, or insects and worms in wood, and so on. The differences in the feeding habits are shown by the size and the shape of the bill in each species.

These buntings •were one of the main pieces of evidence in Darwin's book, *On the Origin of Species*. In it, he put forward the theory of evolution by natural selection, which has had such great influence on the study of the natural world ever since.

BIRDS UNDER THREAT

Sadly, today almost 50 species of the bunting family, including several

▶ **The Galapagos finches** The Large cactus finch (*Geospiza conirostris*) **(1)** is a seed-eater. The Warbler finch (*Certhidae olivacea*) **(2)** picks small insects from trees. The Small ground finch (*Geospiza fulginosa*) **(3)** feeds on small seeds. The Woodpecker finch (*Certhidae pallidus*) **(4)** extracts insects from branches. The Sharp-beaked ground finch (*Geospiza difficilis*) **(5)** eats seeds. The Vegetarian finch (*Platyspiza crassirostris*) **(6)** takes buds and leaves.

▼ Cardinals like wood edges, hedges and suburbs. This is a male; the female is yellow-brown, but still has a crest.

64

buntings, finches, tanagers, saltators and dacnises, are either known, or thought to be, under threat. The main problem is the cutting down of tropical forests in South America so the land can be used to grow crops and raise livestock.

There are a few success stories, however. The Azure-rumped tanager from Mexico and Guatemala was known to science only by three specimens collected for museums – one in the mid-1800s, one in 1937 and one in 1943. It was thought to be extinct. Then in the 1970s observers saw small flocks of this beautiful bird high in the forests of Mexico. This species is on the international wildlife authority's list as "indeterminate." This means that not enough is known about it to put it in one of the categories of "endangered," "vulnerable" or "rare."

Like many island birds, buntings on small islands find it very difficult to survive when cats, dogs, rats and other new predators are introduced by people. Hopefully these birds will not lose out in the struggle for survival.

AMERICAN BLACKBIRDS

On a midwinter's evening, in the southern USA, it looks as though a dark cloud has suddenly appeared and almost blotted out the Sun. But the black, swirling mass is not a cloud. A gigantic flock of American blackbirds, including Common grackles and cowbirds, is returning to its nightly roost, after a day feeding on winter crops in the surrounding fields.

American blackbirds are common and familiar over much of North and South America. The family includes grackles, blackbirds, the bobolink, oropendulas and cowbirds. Outside the breeding season, many species form enormous mixed flocks – some winter roosts in the southern USA have numbered 50 million birds!

Most species in the family are found in the tropics. In Columbia, for example, there are 27 species. These birds prefer mostly open places – prairie and farmland, scrub, scattered woodland and marshes. The female builds the nest, incubates the eggs and feeds the chicks; in some species the male helps with this last task.

TRANS-AMERICAN FLIGHT
Some American blackbirds migrate each year. A sign of spring is the arrival of the bobolink in grassy areas of central North America, having flown from its southern summer in Argentina. On its return journey in the fall, it island-hops across 1,250 miles of sea. Females look as they do all year, their buff-brown plumage speckled with darker brown and black. Males have a similar plumage out of the breeding season, but in spring they exchange it for a bright yellow patch on the back of the neck, white patches on the shoulders and rump, and a black body. This patterning gives them their local name of "skunkbird."

▲ The Common grackle is sometimes a pest in ricefields and cornfields.

UNWANTED VISITORS
Cowbirds, like cuckoos, are brood parasites. They lay their eggs in the nests of other birds, which are the unsuspecting hosts. The hosts then raise the chicks. Some species of cowbirds choose host species with eggs that look similar to their own. Also, they throw out one of the host's eggs for each egg they lay.

▼ Types of blackbird The bobolink (1), Red-winged blackbird (*Agelaius phoeniceus*) (2), Red-breasted blackbird (*Leistes militaris*) (3) and Rusty blackbird (*Euphagus carolinus*) (4).

AMERICAN BLACK-BIRDS Icteridae (*94 species*)

⬙ Diet: seeds, fruit, small animals.

◯ Breeding: 1 or 2 clutches yearly; eggs incubated for 12-15 days.

Size: length 6-21in; weight ⅔-16 ounces.

Plumage: males black with patches of yellow, orange or red; some females and grassland species are brownish.

Species mentioned in text:
Bobolink (*Dolichonyx oryzivorus*)
Bay-winged cowbird (*Molothrus badius*)
Common grackle (*Quiscalus quiscula*)
Screaming cowbird (*Molothrus rufoaxillaris*)
Yellow-headed blackbird (*Xanthocephalus xanthocephalus*)

● ■ 🕱

■ Habitat: grassland, marsh, scrub, patchy wood, forest.

Not all cowbirds do this. The Bay-winged cowbird takes over the nest of another bird, empties it, lays its eggs and rears its own chicks. This species may be visited by a close relative, the Screaming cowbird, which lays an egg and leaves. So one cowbird species raises the chicks of another!

About nine species of American blackbird are thought to be under threat, chiefly in South America and on Caribbean islands. Other species, especially in grain-growing areas of North America, are very common.

▲Like many American blackbirds, the Yellow-headed blackbirds gather in large flocks outside the breeding season.

◀American blackbirds find much of their food by "gaping." The bird pushes its closed bill into a hollow stem or other likely place, and then opens its bill to split the stem. This reveals small creatures such as insects and spiders, which the bird would not otherwise be able to see.

FINCHES

On a warm tropical evening in the Hawaiian Islands, a flock of apapanes flies over. Their dazzling orange plumage matches the rays of the setting Sun. They have spent the day probing flowers for nectar with their long, delicate beaks, and are now flying home to their roost.

FINCHES Fringillidae
(*153 species*)

● ◧ ∱

◿ Habitat: woods, forest, parks.

■ Diet: seeds, nuts and berries, some insects; also nectar.

◎ Breeding: average 1 or 2 clutches per year, each 3-5 eggs; incubation 12-14 days.

Size: length 4-10in; weight ⅓-3 ounces.

Plumage: varied in color, usually with striking wing or tail markings.

Species mentioned in text:
American goldfinch (*Carduelis tristis*)
Apapane (*Himatione sanguinea*)
Brambling (*Fringilla montifringilla*)
Bullfinch (*Pyrrhula pyrrhula*)
Chaffinch (*Fringilla coelebs*)
Crossbills (genus *Loxia*)
European goldfinch (*Carduelis carduelis*)
Greenfinch (*C. chloris*)
Laysan finch (*Telespyza cantans*)
Linnet (*Acanthis cannabina*)
Nihoa finch (*Telespyza ultima*)

A problem with the name "finch" is that it is often given to any smallish or medium-sized bird with a stout, cone-shaped bill used for crushing seeds. Yet not all finches belong to the "true" finch family, Fringillidae, described here. For example, the small seed-eating and insect-eating birds of the Galapagos Islands are known as Galapagos finches, but they belong to the bunting family (see page 64).

WHAT IS A FINCH?
The true finch family also includes the Hawaiian finches, which live on various islands of the Hawaii group, in the Pacific. Some of these Hawaiian finches are called honeycreepers but birds from other families are also called honeycreepers, such as (once more) certain buntings (see page 60).

This confusion shows the importance of scientific (Latin) names for species and groups of animals. The scientific name for each species is the same throughout the world, and is unique for that species, so there can be no mix-up.

CROSS-OVER BILL
Some of the strangest bills in the bird world belong to the crossbills. The two parts of the bill cross over at the tip, like a pair of bent pliers. The bill is used to lever open the scales on the cones of various conifer trees, to reach the seeds underneath.

Like many finches, crossbills tend to breed whenever food is abundant. In larch forests, this is mainly in late summer or early in fall. In spruce forests, it is in late fall to winter, and in pine forests it is in spring. In areas where various types of conifer grow, crossbills may breed for 10 months of the year – including mid-winter, when hardly any other birds are nesting. Near Moscow, USSR, crossbill nests were found in February, when the air temperature was −2°F! Yet inside the nest, as the female sat on her eggs, it was a snug 100°F.

▼The chaffinch (this one is a male) is the commonest bird in many parts of Europe and is a familiar sight in woods, gardens and parks.

►▼Heads and bills of finches The hawfinch (*Coccothraustes cocco-thraustes*) **(1)**, which has a massive bill for cracking large seeds and nuts. The siskin (*C. spinus*) **(2)**, European goldfinch **(3)**, ou (*Psittirostra psittacea*) **(4)** and Two-barred crossbill (*Loxia leucoptera*) **(5)**. The apapane **(6)**, a nectar-eater from Hawaii, has a thin bill for probing into flowers. The Parrot crossbill (*Loxia pytopsittacus*) **(7)** tackles the hard cones of pine trees.

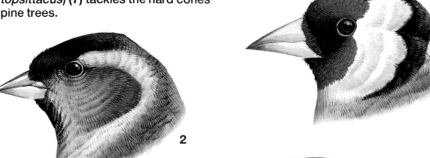

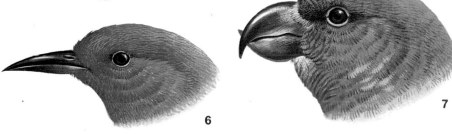

Other finches which breed as food (mainly seeds) becomes available include the greenfinch, linnet and bullfinch. They can nest and raise young from early spring to midsummer. The European goldfinch, which likes the seeds of thistles and similar plants, breeds later in summer. The American goldfinch, which depends even more on thistles, breeds even later in the year. The average start of its breeding season is the latest of all the birds in North America.

THE COMMONEST BIRDS...
The finch family includes such common and well-known species as the chaffinch, greenfinch and European goldfinch, each of which often comes into parks and gardens to feed. These colorful and active birds, with their chirpy, twittering songs, are favorites with birdwatchers, and they are also very familiar to many people who know little about birds.

The chaffinch, in particular, is one of the commonest birds in Europe. In some areas of wood and scrub, one bird in every four is a chaffinch. It is

▼Some finches are common visitors to feeders, and people have devised tests to see if they are "intelligent." After a few tries, this European goldfinch worked out how to lift the string with its bill, hold the loop with its feet, and do this several times in order to lift the food on to the twig.

thought that there are as many as 12 million of these birds in Britain.

Bramblings, too, are common over much of Northern Europe and Asia. They gather in huge flocks where food such as berries, seeds, and especially beechmast (beech "nuts") is plentiful. Some bramblings migrate to Britain in winter, where they join their finch cousins in mixed flocks, foraging for seeds and nuts in woods, hedgerows, parks and farmland.

...AND THE RAREST
At the other end of the scale, some of the Hawaiian finches are among the rarest birds in the world. Of the 28 species identified by scientists in recent times, 8 have died out completely and 16 more are probably threatened with extinction.

Like the Galapagos finches, it is thought that the Hawaiian finches evolved over thousands or millions of years from one original finch species. This "ancestral species" probably resembled the Nihoa finch of today. It crossed some 1,800 miles of ocean to reach the Hawaiian Islands. Here it found a lot of different habitats, from coral reefs to lowland woods and mountain rain forests. Also, the islands were remote, and had formed relatively recently, so there were few other birds and animals to compete with the finch for food or nesting sites. In such conditions, evolution could happen rapidly.

Years ago, rabbits were brought to Laysan, one of the Hawaiian Islands. It was hoped they could be farmed for meat. Sadly they ate so much vegetation that by the 1920s they had turned the island almost into a desert. The Laysan honeycreeper, an island sub-species of the apapane, became extremely rare. After a great storm in 1923, which swept sand and dust over

▲ A crossbill male regurgitates a meal of seeds for its young. The nestlings have streaked plumage, while their parents have blotchy feathers.

▶ A Laysan finch perches, its short, tough bill and long tail feathers clearly visible.

the island non-stop for 3 days, this honeycreeper disappeared for ever.

Today, there are several threats to the survival of the Hawaiian finches. These include destruction of their habitats by people and their animals (chiefly cattle, goats and pigs), predators such as cats brought by people, and diseases brought by new animals and birds. These threats have greatly reduced the numbers of all the remaining Hawaiian finch species. It is to be hoped that conservation efforts now under way will protect most of the species still alive, saving these beautiful birds from extinction.

WAXBILLS

A flock of Gouldian finches swoops through the scrub of the Australian outback. Suddenly the birds fly into a fine-mesh "mist net" strung in the bushes, and are entangled. The net is the work of poachers who want to sell the birds abroad – against the law. Luckily, wildlife officers are tracking the poachers, and the catchers are caught.

Waxbills (not to be confused with waxwings, page 58) are mostly small-ish, grain-eating birds from central and southern Africa, southern and South-east Asia and the Australian region. Because of their stocky build and stout, seed-crushing bills, some of them are called finches, although they are not "true" finches (see page 68).

Outside the breeding season, many waxbill species form large flocks. The birds take off, whirl around and land in a close-knit group, moving with great co-ordination, as if joined by pieces of elastic. Research has shown that calls given by members of the flock, and the sight of other birds moving about, helps to keep the birds together.

EGGS AND CHICKS IN DANGER

During the rainy season, males and females pair off. They show many types of courtship behavior, such as preening each other. Or the male may pick up a piece of nesting material such as a grass stem and hop around the female, singing and waving the stem in front of her.

▶ Types of waxbill A piebald form of the domesticated Bengalese finch (1), Zebra finch (2), Blue-faced parrot finch (*Erythrura trichroa*) (3), Violet-eared waxbill (*Uraeginthus granatinus*) (4), waxbill (*Estrilda astrild*) (5), White-backed munia (6).

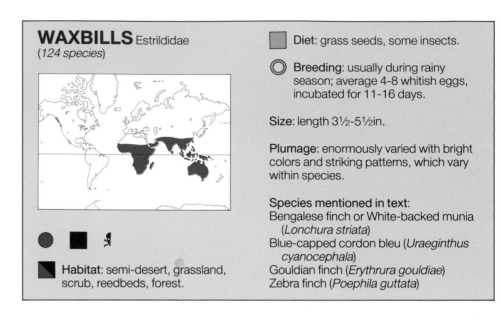

WAXBILLS Estrildidae
(*124 species*)

■ Diet: grass seeds, some insects.

◎ Breeding: usually during rainy season; average 4-8 whitish eggs, incubated for 11-16 days.

Size: length 3½-5½in.

Plumage: enormously varied with bright colors and striking patterns, which vary within species.

Species mentioned in text:
Bengalese finch or White-backed munia (*Lonchura striata*)
Blue-capped cordon bleu (*Uraeginthus cyanocephala*)
Gouldian finch (*Erythrura gouldiae*)
Zebra finch (*Poephila guttata*)

● ■ ☠

◨ Habitat: semi-desert, grassland, scrub, reedbeds, forest.

Most waxbills make a dome-shaped nest with a side entrance, built from grass and other soft material. The chicks are fed on seeds from grasses and other plants, and on insects and other small creatures. Predators such as hawks, snakes and rats take as many as four out of five eggs, and also destroy numerous nestlings. However, if they are left alone in the wild, waxbills seem able to keep up their numbers – but they are not always left alone, as explained below.

COLORFUL CAGEBIRDS

Waxbills are perhaps best known for their extraordinary plumage. They wear some of the brightest colors and patterns in the bird world. This, in addition to their pleasing song, has made them popular as cagebirds.

Two species of waxbills in particular, the Bengalese finch and the Zebra finch, are now fully domesticated. They have been bred to give a number of color varieties. These and other species, such as the cordon bleus and firefinches, are kept by bird breeders throughout the world.

▼ The Blue-capped cordon bleu is found throughout East Africa. Like many waxbills, it is a favorite with cagebird enthusiasts.

▲ The extraordinary colors of the Gouldian finch makes it look like a "painting-by-numbers" bird.

Some of the birds kept in cages have been supplied by dealers who caught them in the wild, in Africa and Asia. More than seven million birds are imported to Europe each year, and a very large proportion of these are wild-caught waxbills.

In the 1960s the Australian government made laws to prevent import or export of many animals, including waxbills. This meant cagebird breeders there could no longer bring in foreign species. However, they were able to breed foreign birds already in their country, such as cordon bleus and firefinches, which they did successfully. So perhaps some of the international trade in waxbills, as in other creatures, is not necessary.

A few waxbill species are numerous, and trapping has had little effect on their numbers – as yet. But it is thought that other species are becoming rarer. Also, some dealers do not care for their birds and many die on the journey, through overcrowding or lack of food or water. Eight species of the waxbill family are thought to be at risk and are listed in the 1988 IUCN Red List of Threatened Animals.

WEAVERS

1

A snake slithers up a tree on the dry African grassland. Attracted by the noise of birds nesting in the branches, it is after a nestling. As the snake reaches the nests, it finds each one made of thorns, with a downwards-pointing tunnel. When the snake tries to enter, it falls to the ground.

WEAVERS Ploceidae
(*143 species*)

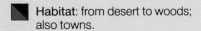

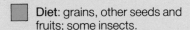

Habitat: from desert to woods; also towns.

Diet: grains, other seeds and fruits; some insects.

Breeding: 2-7 eggs per clutch: incubation 9-20 days.

Size: length 4½-26in (most 6-10in).

Plumage: mostly browns and grays with black, dark or light brown streaks, mainly on wings.

Species mentioned in text:
Baya weaver (*Ploceus philippinus*)
Bishops (genus *Euplectes*)
Cassin's weaver (*Malimbus cassini*)
House sparrow (*Passer domesticus*)
Red-billed quelea (*Quelea quelea*)
Red-headed weaver (*Anaplectes rubriceps*)
Rock sparrows (genus *Petronia*)
Snow finches (genus *Montifringilla*)
Tree sparrow (*Passer montanus*)
Village weaver (*Ploceus cucullatus*)
Yellow-throated sparrow (*Petronia xanthocollis*)

Since ancient times, people have been fascinated by the extraordinary nests built by the weaver birds of Africa. These birds are tree-dwellers with bright yellow or red plumage. They make tough, ball-shaped nests from sharp twigs, thorns, grasses and other material, weaving the pieces together with their bills in the way that people weave rugs and thick cloth.

Usually the male fashions the nest and then tries to attract a female to mate and lay eggs there. Many weavers are colonial breeders, and dozens of nests may hang from the outer branches of a particularly suitable tree. In the Village weaver, each male constructs several nests and "advertises" them to any interested females. He hangs upside down at the

▲▶**Types of weaver and sparrow**
A male Golden palm weaver (*Ploceus bojeri*) **(1)** displays at his nest. A House sparrow **(2)** with wings at the bottom of their down stroke. This species has been introduced throughout the world and is now common in North America. A male Golden bishop (*Euplectes afer*) **(3)** ruffles his feathers in courtship flight. A Pin-tailed whydah (*Vidua macroura*) **(4)** perches to show its extraordinary tail feathers. A White-headed buffalo weaver (*Dinemellia dinemellia*) **(5)** with its large, heavy bill. A Social weaver (*Philetairus socius*) **(6)** in front of its colony's nests.

▼Locust-like flocks of Red-billed queleas do enormous damage to grain crops in Africa, despite trapping and poisoning.

entrance to each nest in turn, flapping his wings and chattering loudly.

FORTRESS FOR THE YOUNG
The typical weaver's nest is extremely well protected against predators. It is high in a tree, well out of reach of ground animals. The nest entrance is on the underside, so that climbing animals such as cats and snakes have considerable trouble getting inside to eat the eggs or nestlings.

Some weaver species build an entrance tunnel up to 24in long, for extra protection against climbers and predatory birds. Also, the nests are often sited at the ends of thin twigs or palm fronds, where large and heavy animals cannot climb. And nests are sometimes built on branches overhanging water, to provide further security for the eggs and young.

THE PLAGUE BIRDS
The 94 species of "true" weavers (Ploceinae) are only one group within the weaver family. Other types of true weavers are the bishops, which build

globular nests in grasses or bushes. Weavers generally are thick-set, seed-eating birds with short, strong bills. The males of many species have glossy red, yellow or black plumage. The females all tend to be duller browns, grays and black, streaked and speckled with the same colors.

Also included in the true weavers is the Red-billed quelea, which has been known from the earliest times as a menace to grain crops. This species breeds and feeds in immense flocks, sometimes numbering more than one million birds. In the 1940s it became necessary to attempt to control the numbers of this species in Sudan, Africa, by means such as trapping, shooting and poisoning. Vast numbers of birds have been killed, and the measures continue today – yet so do the plagues of Red-billed queleas.

THE WHYDAH PARASITE
A second group within the weaver family is the viduine weavers and whydahs (Viduinae, nine species). These are "brood parasites," like the

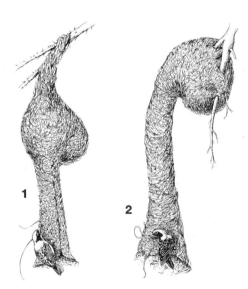

▲ Weavers at work. The amazing woven nests of weaver birds are among the most elaborate in the bird world. Here a Baya weaver (1) and a Cassin's weaver (2) put the finishing touches to the entrance tunnels of their nests.

cuckoos, laying their eggs in the nests of other birds, in this case waxbills. Waxbill chicks have colored marks in their mouths, and when they open their bills, the parent sees the marks and responds by feeding the chicks with regurgitated food. When a whydah chick hatches in a waxbill nest, it too has these colored marks, and the parent feeds it just as if the chick were its own.

A third group of weavers consists of the three species of buffalo weaver (Bubalornithinae) from Africa south of the Sahara. Like many of their weaver cousins, they live in dry areas of grassland with scattered woods and acacia country. They also make large, untidy, domed nests of thorny twigs. Buffalo weavers feed on the ground in the manner of starlings, eating a mixed menu of seeds, fruit and insects.

A BIRD TIED TO PEOPLE
The fourth group of weavers are the sparrows. These familiar birds include the tree sparrows, rock sparrows and snow finches (Passerinae, 37 species). The name "sparrow" is often given to any smallish bird streaked with brown, gray and black, and with a short, thick bill designed for eating seeds. In this way, common names can be confusing, as they are for finches (see page 68). The only way to avoid confusion is to use the scientific (Latin) name for a species.

The House sparrow is one of the most familiar of all birds, rarely found breeding away from people in their farmyards, villages and towns. (At least eight species of sparrow regularly nest in or on inhabited buildings.) These sparrows can exist mainly on bread and household scraps. In many areas they are the commonest of the birds that eat bits of leftover food, which is either thrown on the ground, dumped on refuse heaps or falls from bird tables. Even so, they are very wary and it is difficult to get close to them or keep them in captivity.

VARIED HABITATS
The House sparrow lives mainly in Europe and western Asia, as well as in other regions where it has been taken by people. In eastern Asia, the Tree sparrow is a similarly familiar species, breeding in and near buildings.

Rock sparrows are mainly gray and brown birds with a yellow patch on the throat. However, some species of Rock sparrow, such as the Yellow-throated sparrow (which lives from Africa to India), prefer trees to rocks.

The snow finches spend almost all of their time on the ground. They live on mountains and are among the highest-nesting of all birds – some species breed at heights of more than 14,800ft. In winter, they flock together on lower slopes, searching for seeds and other plant matter, but they never leave the mountains altogether.

PROTECTING A PEST
Although several members of the weaver family are so common, such as the Red-billed quelea and the House sparrow, others are very rare. Some 16 species are under threat according to the international wildlife authority IUCN. They include 12 true weavers on the African continent, 1 in India, and 3 from the islands of Mauritius, Rodrigues and the Seychelles in the Indian Ocean. In some of these areas, the birds are now protected by law.

At one time, even the House sparrow was protected by law. This adaptable bird followed Europeans as they spread to new continents, especially North America and Australia. So that the bird could establish itself, killing it was forbidden. But the sparrow bred so successfully and quickly that it became a pest, and the laws were later done away with and replaced by bounty schemes. But by then it was too late to stop the bird's spread.

▶ A male Red-headed weaver surveys the countryside from the trapeze-like beginnings of the nest he is building.

STARLINGS

At dusk in a large European city, the red sky is darkened by a vast, swirling flock of birds. They land on trees, window ledges and roofs, taking advantage of the lack of predators and the warmth from the buildings. They are starlings – and a problem for the city. Their squawks fill the air and their droppings foul the ground below their roosts.

The European starling is one of the most numerous birds in the world. Many millions of these starlings live across Europe, the Americas and Asia. They are noisy and aggressive birds, and they drive away other species from food and nesting areas.

Roosting flocks in some city-centers contain more than one million starlings. The birds do enormous damage as they fly out by day to raid farmland and eat grapes, olives, cherries, grain crops and cattle food. In the evening they return to city-centers, where they are a noise nuisance and health hazard, polluting buildings and parks with their droppings and feathers. They are also pests in gardens, where they eat all kinds of fruits.

AMERICAN IMPORTS

A century ago, there were no European starlings in North America. In 1890, about 100 of them were released in New York. Today, this species is one of the commonest birds and a major pest on the continent.

Despite this, European starlings are welcomed in some areas. In northern Europe, central Asia and New Zealand they are said to help farmers by eating insects that damage crops.

WALKING WITH A WADDLE

The European starling is a typical member of its family. Starlings generally are small- to medium-sized birds with longish, pointed bills suited for most foods, from worms to wheat.

▲ Types of starling The Hill mynah (1) imitating animal sounds, the Red-billed oxpecker (*Buphagus erythrorhynchus*) (2), and the very rare Rothschild's mynah (*Leucospar rothschildi*) (3) from one small nature reserve in Bali, Indonesia.

Their legs and feet are large and they tend to walk with a waddle, rather than hop.

Some starling species from Southeast Asia have areas of bare skin on the head. At breeding time, the males' skin is often brightly colored yellow, blue or red. In other species there are "wattles" or fleshy lobes on the head. In its breeding plumage, the male Wattled starling, from Africa and the Middle East, has a bare yellow head with black wattles on its chin and forehead.

Starlings usually breed in holes, where they build a bulky, untidy nest. The hole may be in a tree or rock face; some species use nooks and crannies in buildings. The Thin-billed chestnut-winged starling even nests in holes behind waterfalls!

THE "TALKING" BIRD

Many types of starling are good mimics. They can imitate the calls of other birds and also the sounds made by other animals, such as pigs and dogs. The best mimics in the family are the mynahs, which are well known as tame birds that can "talk." In fact the birds do not understand the meaning of what they say – they simply imitate

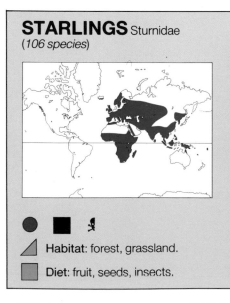

STARLINGS Sturnidae
(*106 species*)

● ■ 🐾

△ Habitat: forest, grassland.

▨ Diet: fruit, seeds, insects.

◎ Breeding: usually 1 clutch per year; 1-6 eggs, pale blue with brownish spots in most species; incubation 11-18 days.

Size: length 6-18in; weight 1½-6 ounces.

Plumage: chiefly dark with green, purple and blue sheens; some species are gray, brilliant orange or yellow.

Species mentioned in text:
Common mynah (*Acridotheres tristis*)
European starling (*Sturnus vulgaris*)
Hill mynah (*Gracula religiosa*)
Thin-billed chestnut-winged starling
   (*Onychognathus tenuirostris*)
Wattled starling (*Creatophora conerea*)

human speech in the same way that they copy animal noises. The cagebird kept for mimicry is most commonly the Hill mynah.

ON THE LOOK-OUT
The starling family also includes birds known as oxpeckers. These perch on a large animal, such as a buffalo or antelope, and peck at the flies and other small creatures which live in and on the animal's fur. The large animal benefits by losing irritating pests, while the oxpecker gets a good and easy meal.

Despite the huge numbers of some starlings, seven species in the family are thought to be under threat from habitat destruction or being killed for food. Of these, five live on islands, including Bali, the Cook Islands and the Solomon Islands.

▲A male European starling pauses on his perch before flying a few yards to feed his young in their tree-hole nest.

▼A Common mynah feeds a caterpillar to its young in a New Zealand forest, where this species has been introduced.

BOWERBIRDS

In a warm, wet forest in northeast Australia, a glossy male Satin bowerbird dances and calls in front of his bower – an avenue lined with upright twigs and sticks. At one end, a patch of cleared ground is strewn with feathers, shells and similar natural trinkets.

Bowerbirds are extraordinary artists and builders. The males clear a patch or "court" of ground and place there brightly-colored objects, from berries and fruits to leaves, feathers, cast-off insect skins and the wings of butterflies. Artificial objects, such as bits of tinfoil and plastic, bottletops, buttons and coins have also been found at bowerbird courts.

In many species, the male also constructs an elaborate bower from twigs, sticks, leaves and moss. (The word "bower" means a shady, leafy shelter – and also a lady's bedroom!) He may "decorate" the bower with shiny objects, flowers and leaves. In a few species the male even "paints" the bower with a natural colored substance, such as the juice from a fruit, using a scrap of bark as a brush.

Studies on Satin bowerbirds seem to show that the male must learn how to build his bower – the skills are not present in the young birds.

IMPRESSING THE FEMALES

The reason for all this activity is to impress females of the species. The male Satin bowerbird, for example, attracts a female with grating, cackling and squeaking calls. He dances about with his tail cocked high, jumps over the bower and points his bill at the collection of "decorations." In this way he attracts and mates with as many females as possible. Then the females go off to build a nest, incubate the eggs and raise the chicks. The male plays no part in raising the young.

FOUR TYPES OF BOWER

There are four main types of bower. One is the simple court, a cleared patch of ground decorated only with

▼Types of bower. The "avenue" of the Satin bowerbird (1), the cave-like bower of the Striped gardener (2), the stick tower of MacGregor's gardener (3), and the thatched hut of the Vogelkop gardener (4).

BOWERBIRDS
Ptilonorhynchidae (*18 species*)

▲ **Habitat**: rain forest, woods, grassland, dry scrub.

▨ **Diet**: fruit, insects and small animals, lizards, nestlings.

◎ **Breeding**: 1 or 2 (rarely 3) eggs per clutch; incubation 19-24 days.

Size: length 8½-15in; weight 2½-8 ounces.

Plumage: nine species camouflaged mainly in greens, browns and grays; males of other species with patches of bright yellow, red or blue.

Species mentioned in text:
Adelbert bowerbird (*Sericulus bakeri*)
Archbold's bowerbird (*Archboldia papuensis*)
MacGregor's gardener (*Amblyornis macgregoriae*)
Satin bowerbird (*Ptilonorhynchus violaceus*)
Spotted bowerbird (*Chlamydera maculata*)
Striped gardener (*Amblyornis subalaris*)
Vogelkop gardener (*A. inornatus*)

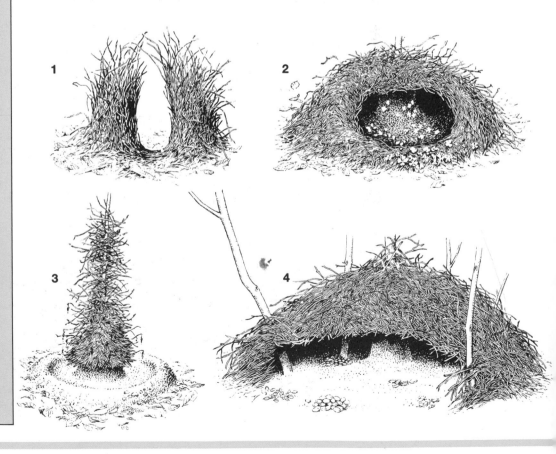

leaves. Another is the mat, a carpet of mosses and ferns, as made by Archbold's bowerbird. A third type is the avenue of the Satin and the Spotted bowerbirds – a cleared area in front of two parallel stick-and-twig walls. The fourth type is the "maypole" of the gardener bowerbirds, in which all manner of items are piled around a thin tree trunk.

In general, the brighter and more colorful species of bowerbirds build small, simple bowers. Dull males, that are lacking in crests or other colorful plumage (Vogelkop's gardener, for instance) make the most elaborate and attractive bowers.

FOOD AND FORESTS
Bowerbirds are, as a rule, rather stout, medium-sized birds with strong feet and heavy bills. They eat a variety of foods. In winter some of the avenue-building species form flocks which may damage fruit crops.

Most bowerbirds live in warm, wet forests. There are nine species in New Guinea, seven in Australia, and two in both regions. Archbold's bowerbird was first sighted in 1940, 13,200ft up in the rain forests of Papua New Guinea. One species, the Adelbert bowerbird (also from Papua New Guinea), is thought to be rare and possibly at risk of dying out. This is mainly because distribution is patchy, making it difficult to find a mate.

▲A Spotted bowerbird from Australia catches an insect. This species lives in grassland and dry woodland and builds the "avenue" type of bower.

▼A male Satin bowerbird collects objects near his bower to impress the female, including green leaves, blue feathers – and a blue plastic lid!

BIRDS OF PARADISE

In 1522, the surviving ship of Magellan's round-the-world expedition returned to Spain. It bore presents from a ruler of the Molucca Islands – feathers of exotic shapes and brilliant colors. Spaniards could not believe that such beauty came from forests in South-east Asia. They thought the feathers came from paradise – and so these birds were named.

Male birds of paradise are famous for their bizarre and exotic appearance. They have fantastic feather structures, such as long and elegant plumes, batches of fluffy feathers like feather-dusters, and narrow quill-like "wires" on the head or tail. Colors vary from glossy black to grays and browns, with brilliant shining patches of rich reds, greens and blues, and warmly glowing pastel shades.

NATURE'S SHOW-OFFS

The purpose of the male's plumage is to impress females of his species, and attract them in order to mate. In some species, such as the Blue bird of paradise, several males may gather at a traditional place called a lek. Here they display to attract females and show their superiority over other males. They jump about on a perch, call loudly, spread their feathers to show off their shapes and colors, rock to and fro, and even hang upside down, shimmering their wings and tail. Such sights are among the most exciting in the natural world.

In other species, males display on their own, at traditional "courts" or perches in the forest. Younger males, in drabber, female-like plumage, look on and wait for the opportunity to occupy the perch. They may spend up

▶The Raggiana bird of paradise spreads his amazing plumage; in his courtship display, he also hangs upside down.

BIRDS OF PARADISE
Paradisaeidae (*43 species*)

● ◩ 🏴

◿ **Habitat:** various types of forest, mangrove woods and swamps.

◿ **Diet:** fruit; some species also take insects and other small animals, leaves, buds, flowers.

○ **Breeding:** 1 or 2 (rarely 3) eggs per clutch, pale with colorful spots and blotches, smudged at large end; incubation 17-21 days.

Size: length 6-44in, mostly 10-20in.

Plumage: most males are very colorful with ornate feathers; most females are camouflaged in browns and greens.

Species mentioned in text:
Blue bird of paradise (*Paradisaea rudolphi*)
King bird of paradise (*Cicinnurus regius*)
MacGregor's bird of paradise (*Macgregoria pulchra*)
Manucodes (genus *Manucodia*)
Raggiana bird of paradise (*Paradisaea raggiana*)
Riflebirds (genus *Ptiloris*)
Sicklebills (genus *Epimachus*)

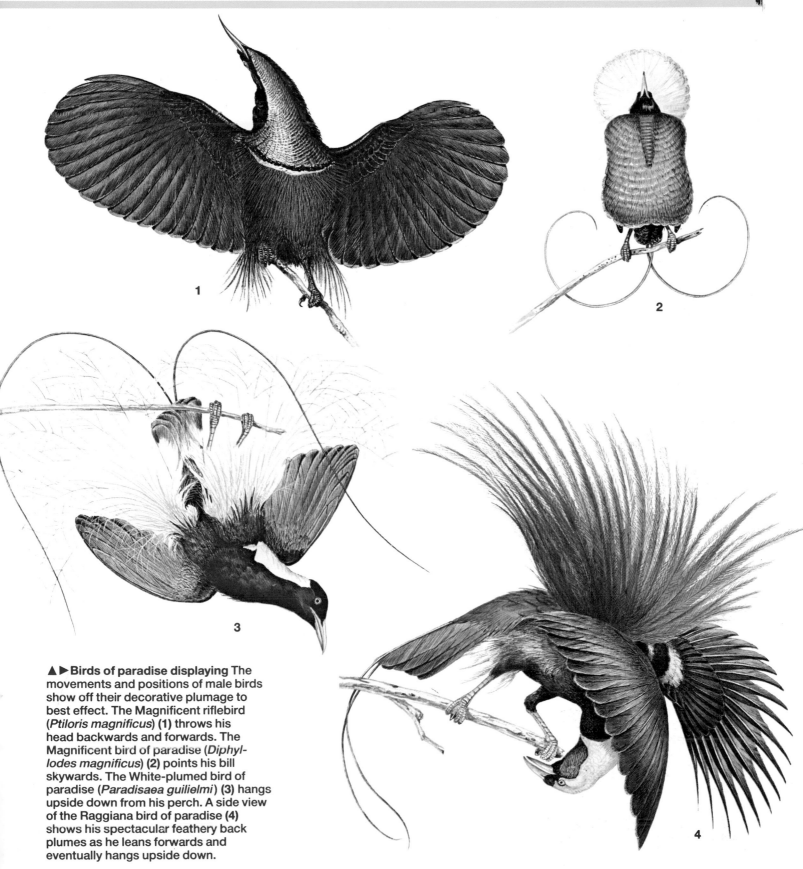

▲▶**Birds of paradise displaying** The movements and positions of male birds show off their decorative plumage to best effect. The Magnificent riflebird (*Ptiloris magnificus*) **(1)** throws his head backwards and forwards. The Magnificent bird of paradise (*Diphyllodes magnificus*) **(2)** points his bill skywards. The White-plumed bird of paradise (*Paradisaea guilielmi*) **(3)** hangs upside down from his perch. A side view of the Raggiana bird of paradise **(4)** shows his spectacular feathery back plumes as he leans forwards and eventually hangs upside down.

to 6 or 7 years before they become mature and take center stage.

The extraordinary colors, feathers and courtship behavior of the male birds of paradise are believed to have evolved through "sexual selection." Females are thought to choose the most colorful and splendid male, so his characteristics (in the form of genes) will be passed on to the next generation. Rather than survival of the fittest, it is success of the showiest.

FATHERLESS BROOD
When the females have mated, they leave to raise the young. Males take no further part in breeding. In most species, the female's plumage is drab brown, green or gray, providing good camouflage in the dim light among the forest vegetation.

The female builds a bulky bowl-shaped nest from leaves and trailing tendrils, on a foundation of sticks and twigs. The nest is usually hidden in a tree or vine. Several species construct domed nests, while the King bird of paradise nests in holes.

PARADISE CAN BE DULL
Not all male birds of paradise have amazingly colorful plumage. About nine species are much duller, and the males and females look similar. They include the five species of blue-black manucodes and the generally black MacGregor's bird of paradise.

Most birds of paradise live in Papua New Guinea, although four species also occur in north-eastern Australia, and two live in Maluku (formerly the Moluccan Islands). They are generally stout birds, varying from starling-sized to crow-sized, with rounded wings and very strong feet.

SWORDS AND SICKLES
Bill shapes vary within the family. Some species have longish, sword-like bills for eating a variety of foods such as fruits, seeds and small creatures. The sicklebills and riflebirds have long, thin, curved bills suited to probing under moss and bark for insects, worms and grubs. The rifle-birds are so named because the male's two-part call sounds like the whistle of a rifle bullet.

The main habitat of birds of paradise is damp forest, from the warm tropical lowlands to the cooler uplands and mountains. A few species live in mangrove woods and swamps or in lowland savannah.

ISLANDS IN THE LOWLANDS
Threats to the survival of the birds of paradise arise partly because the different species live in different mountain ranges. Once their own area is disturbed – usually by clearing for agriculture or felling trees for timber – they are unable to move the long distances to other suitable habitats. In this respect they resemble threatened species on oceanic islands, such as the Hawaiian finches (see page 70). Birds of paradise can be thought of as marooned on mountainous islands in a sea of unsuitable lowland habitats. Threatened species include the Blue bird of paradise, whose mountain forests are shrinking rapidly as they are felled for farmland.

In the past, birds of paradise were killed and their beautiful feathers sent overseas, to adorn the hats and gowns of the rich. Today some hunting still continues by local peoples, who use the feathers to decorate ceremonial head-dresses.

Some species in the remote mountain forest of Irian Jaya (Indonesian New Guinea) have not yet been well studied and may be also under serious threat. However, eight species in the family are now regarded as definitely being in need of protection and are likely to be given official conservation status in the near future.

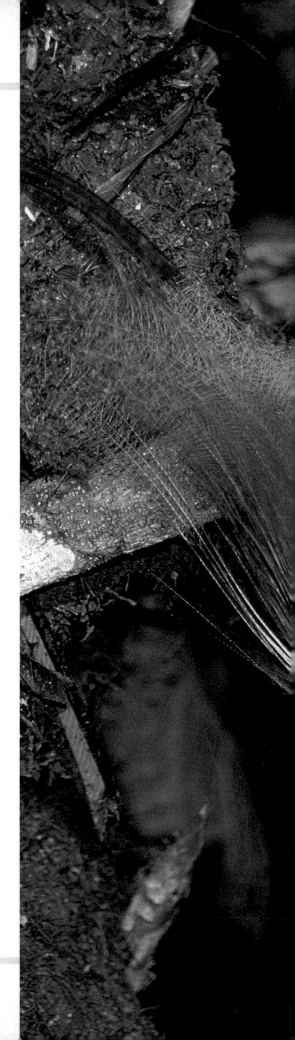

►The electric, shimmering blues and greens of the Blue bird of paradise glow in the dim forest interior.

CROWS

Winter in northern Canada, and a Gray jay lands in a spruce tree to feed. In the fall the jay hid a store of seeds here, sticking them in a tuft of spruce leaves with its own saliva. Now it returns for a mid-winter feast.

CROWS Corvidae (*116 species*)

● ■ ⚶

■ **Habitat:** from desert to tundra.

◪ **Diet:** fruit, seeds, insects, other small animals, eggs, carrion.

◎ **Breeding:** usually 1 clutch per year, 2-8 pale eggs with darker marks; incubation 16-22 days.

Size: length 6-26in; weight 3 ounces-3¼lb.

Plumage: all black, or black marked with white or gray; many jays brightly marked with blue, chestnut or green.

Species mentioned in text:
Azure-winged magpie (*Cyanopica cyana*)
Carrion crow (*Corvus corone*)
Clark's nutcracker (*Nucifraga columbiana*)
European jay (*Garrulus glandarius*)
European nutcracker (*Nucifraga caryocatactes*)
Gray jay (*Perisoreus canadensis*)
Green magpie (*Cissa chinensis*)
Jackdaw (*Corvus monedula*)
Pied crow (*C. albus*)
Raven (*C. corax*)
Rook (*C. frugilegus*)
Scrub jay (*Aphelocoma coerulescens*)

The crow family includes the adaptable crows themselves, and also the jays, magpies, the raven and the rook. These large birds, with their mainly black or dark plumage, and their eerie croaking and cawing calls, have long been said to bring bad luck.

SUPERSTITIONS AND STORIES

Although there is no real scientific evidence for such superstitions, in past times the stories may not have seemed so strange. Crows and ravens are quick to take advantage of new foods, and they feed on carrion (dead animal carcasses). In medieval times, the human corpses from hangings and executions provided a feast for these birds. They were thought to be sent by evil spirits, to peck at and pay back the human victims for crimes they had committed.

▼The European jay is one of many crows that stores food for the winter. This species is especially fond of acorns.

The raven is the world's largest species of passerine (perching birds, in the order Passeriformes). Crows are generally medium-sized to large birds, with robust bodies, powerful legs and feet, and long, strong bills. Many species prefer woodland or forest, and most of the jays and magpies of Asia and South America are limited to forest. The more familiar species of Europe and North America prefer open country, and there are no forest species in Africa or Australia.

THE CLEVER CROWS

Experts regard the crows as the most highly evolved, adaptable and intelligent of all birds. Many stories exist of how they use their wits to survive and find food in almost any habitat, from forest to freezing tundra, hot deserts and busy cities.

▶In winter, times are hard for rooks, just as for other birds. They gather in mixed flocks on open land to feed.

Experiments with jackdaws and ravens have shown that there is a scientific basis to the stories of clever crows. Under certain conditions these birds can "count" up to five or six. They do far better than parrots, chickens and pigeons in tests designed to assess intelligence.

In the wild, the Carrion crow has been observed learning how to open mussels. Individuals plucked these shellfish from the shore, flew up and dropped them on to rocks, cracking the shells. They then flew down, pecked open the broken shells and ate the soft flesh inside. Herring gulls, which are also thought of as intelligent birds, copied the crows. However,

▼**Types of crow** The White-necked raven (*Corvus albicollis*) (**1**), jackdaw (**2**), chough (*Pyrrhocorax pyrrhocorax*) (**3**), magpie (*Pica pica*) (**4**), raven (**5**), European nutcracker (**6**), European jay (**7**), Steller's jay (*Cyanocitta stelleri*) (**8**), Green magpie (**9**) and Red-billed blue magpie (*Urocissa erythrorhyncha*) (**10**).

they did not learn to drop the mussels on a hard surface – they dropped them on soft mud instead!

SQUIRREL-LIKE BEHAVIOR

The crow's powerful build and strong bill allows it to eat most types of food. Seeds, nuts, worms, insects, small animals, eggs and nestlings are all taken as they become available, as well as carrion.

Within the family are two species of nutcracker, which feed largely on the seeds of nuts. These are the Clark's nutcracker of North America and the

▲The Pied crow is common across tropical and southern Africa, and is the only family member found on the island of Madagascar.

◄In winter and early spring, the rook fans its tail and bows, making the "caw" call typical of a rookery (1). Before mating, the wings are arched and tail fanned (2). The rook defends food it has found by the aggressive "take-off" posture with bill pointing upwards (3).

▼The Azure-winged magpie lives in Portugal and Spain and in the Far East – but not in places between.

European nutcracker of Eurasia. The European nutcracker relies mainly on hazelnuts, pine seeds and acorns. It is one of many crow species that store food, such as nuts and berries. This is usually done during the fall, when food is plentiful. Wild jays and crows usually hide their food in small holes, under twigs or vegetation. The food is recovered and eaten during times of hardship, generally during winter.

These birds again reveal their intelligence by having good memories for where their food is hidden. In the winter, nutcrackers have been seen to

dig through snow 8in deep and find hidden food. In the spring, European jays unearth acorns they had hidden and "planted" the previous fall, locating them by the shoots growing from the acorns.

There are also several records of nutcrackers feeding hazelnuts to their nestlings in spring. Presumably these were nuts hidden by the parents during the fall, since all the exposed hazelnuts had long since been eaten by birds and other hungry animals.

THE SOCIABLE ROOKS
A few crow species breed in colonies. Rooks construct bulky, stick-and-twig nests high in trees. Some rookeries

▼ These Carrion crows are doing what their name implies – feeding on carrion, in this case a dead calf on a hillside.

have contained more than 6,000 nests. Jackdaws nest in looser colonies, in holes in trees and rock faces, in disused buildings in city centers, as well as in chimneys and rabbit burrows!

However, pairs of most crows try to set up their own breeding territory. Both male and female defend the territory from intruders of their own species. The female incubates the eggs (except in the nutcrackers, where both parents do so), and the male feeds his partner at this time. Male and female feed the young as nestlings, and also when they leave the nest as fledglings.

In some species the young stay in their parents' territory for several months after they can fend for themselves. In the Scrub jay, from Florida, offspring remain with their parents for a year or more.

NOT ALL DARK-FEATHERED
Not all crows have mainly black or dark plumage. The magpies of southern Asia, such as the Green magpie, have beautifully colored plumage in greens, blues and lilacs, with extraordinary long tail feathers that may be twice the length of the body.

THREATENED CROWS
Today, at least 13 species of crow are considered to be under threat. These rare crows come mainly from Central and South America, eastern Asia, and islands such as Sri Lanka in the Indian Ocean and the Mariana Islands of the western Pacific.

Besides destruction of their forest homes, threats to the survival of some species are introduced members of their own family. Some of these are pests of agriculture too.

GLOSSARY

Aggression Any behavior in which one animal attacks or threatens another.

Air sacs Little air-filled bags in a bird's body connected to its lungs that increase the amount of air a bird breathes in.

Aves The class of animals to which all birds belong.

Avian Relating to birds.

Bill Also called beak; the horny part of a bird's mouth with which it gathers food.

Brood The group of young raised in a single breeding cycle.

Call The sounds a bird makes.

Camouflage Color and patterns on an animal's coat that allow it to blend in with its surroundings.

Canopy The more or less continuous leafy layer of the trees in a wood or forest.

Carrion Meat from a dead animal.

Class The division of animal classification above Order. All birds belong to the class Aves.

Clutch The eggs a bird lays in one breeding session.

Competition The contest between two or more species over such things as space and food.

Conservation Preserving and protecting living things, their habitat and the environment in general.

Courtship The period when an animal tries to attract a mate, or renews its bonds with a mate from previous years.

Crest A set of long feathers on the head of a bird.

Display A typical pattern of behavior associated with important aspects of an animal's life, such as courtship, mating, nesting and defending territory.

Diurnal Active during the day.

Endangered species One whose numbers have dropped so low that it is in danger of becoming extinct.

Environment The surroundings, of a particular species, or the world about us in general.

Extinction The complete loss of a species, either locally or on the Earth.

Family The division of animal classification below Order and above Genus. In the bird world there are 163 recognized families.

Fledging The time when a young bird first takes to the air; a fledgling is a bird that has just begun to fly.

Flight feathers The large feathers on the wings, which are divided into the primaries and secondaries.

Flock A large group of birds whose members habitually move around together.

Foraging Going in search of food.

Frugivores Animals that live chiefly on fruit.

Game birds Birds such as pheasants, grouse, guinea fowl and turkeys, which are hunted for sport or food.

Genus The division of animal classification below Family and above Species. In the bird world there are 1,975 recognized genera.

Gizzard The muscular forepart of a bird's stomach in which hard food is ground; well developed in seed-eating birds such as finches.

Habitat The type of surroundings in which an animal lives.

Hatching The moment when a young bird emerges from the egg; hence *hatchling*, a young bird that has recently hatched.

Home range The area in which an animal usually lives and feeds.

Incubation The period during which a bird sits on a clutch of eggs to keep them warm so that they will develop and eventually hatch.

Insectivores Animals that live chiefly on insects.

Invertebrates Animals without backbones, such as insects and worms. They are a source of food for many birds.

Lek An area of ground where some birds display.

Mammals Animals whose females have mammary glands, which produce milk on which they feed their young. Small mammals are food for some birds.

Mandibles The two parts that make up a bird's bill.

Migration The long-distance movement of animals. It is typically seasonal, e.g. between far northern breeding grounds in summer and warmer southern regions in winter.

Milk A fluid produced in the crop of pigeons (and flamingos), which the birds use to feed their newly hatched young. It has much the same food value as mammal milk.

Mimicry Imitation. Some defenseless animals resemble poisonous or distasteful species in their form or behavior to avoid being preyed upon. Mockingbirds, for example, tend to mimic the sounds of other birds and other noises.

Molt The period during which a bird sheds old feathers and grows new ones.

Monogamous Having only one mate. Some birds stay paired for life. Others just for a breeding season. *Contrast* polygamous.

Nestling A young bird in the nest.

Nocturnal Active during the night.

Nomadic Wandering; having no fixed home territory. Waxwings appear to be nomads, nesting each year where the food is most plentiful.

Omnivore An animal that has a varied diet, eating both plants and animals.

Order The division of animal classification below Class and above Family. There are 28 recognized orders in the bird world.

Passerines Perching birds – those belonging to the order Passeriformes. They include many of our best-known garden birds – flycatchers, swallows, wrens, thrushes, tits, finches, warblers, sparrows, starlings and crows, as well as the highly colored orioles and birds of paradise.

Plumage The feathers of a bird. Many birds have a different plumage in the spring and summer breeding season from that in the winter. The breeding plumage is often vivid, the winter plumage dull.

Polygamous An animal that has more than one mate; most often this applies to males.

Population A separate group of animals of the same species.

Predator An animal that hunts and kills other animals, its prey.

Preening Running the bill through the feathers to keep the plumage clean and airworthy. The action also distributes oil onto the plumage from a preen gland just above the tail.

Primaries The long outer flight feathers on the wings, with which a bird propels itself through the air.

Race The division of animal classification below Sub-species; it refers to animals that are similar but have slightly different characteristics

Ratites Ostriches and their relatives, such as emus, cassowaries and rheas.

Regurgitate Bring up food previously swallowed.

Resident An animal that stays in the same area all year round.

Roosting Sleeping or resting.

Savannah Tropical grassland, particularly in Africa.

Scrape A hollow in the ground made by an animal in which it lays its eggs.

Secondaries The shorter inner flight feathers on the wing, which provide the lift that keeps a bird in the air.

Sibling A "brother" or "sister." In some bird species young remain with their parents when they breed again and look after their younger siblings.

Solitary Mostly living alone.

Species The division of animal classification below Genus; a group of animals of the same structure that can breed together.

Spur A sharp projection on the legs of some birds, used for fighting.

Sub-species The division of animal classification below Species and above Race; typically the sub-species are separated geographically.

Sub-tropics The two warm regions bordering the tropics to the north and south of the equator.

Temperate A climate that is not too hot and not too cold. Temperate zones lie between the sub-tropics and the cold high latitude regions in both hemispheres.

Territory The area in which an animal or group of animals lives and defends against intruders.

Tropics Strictly, the region between latitudes 23° north and south of the equator. Tropical regions are typically very hot and humid.

Tundra The landscape at high latitudes where the very cold climate prevents the growth of trees. A similar habitat occurs at high altitudes on mountains.

Vertebrates Animals with backbones. Fish are aquatic vertebrates and birds are terrestrial vertebrates.

Wattles Fleshy growths on the head of some birds, usually near the base of the bill. They may be highly colored.

INDEX

Common names

Single page numbers indicate a major section of the main text. Double, hyphenated, numbers refer to major articles. **Bold numbers** refer to illustrations.

amazons 35
apapane 68, **69**
aracari
   Collared **48**
aracaris 50, 51
   see also aracari
argus
   Crested 16, **20**

bellbirds 54
bird of paradise
   Blue 82, **84**
   King 84
   MacGregor's 84
   Magnificent **83**
   Raggiana **82**, **83**
   White-plumed **83**
birds of paradise 82-85
   see also bird of paradise, manucodes, riflebirds, sicklebirds
bishop
   Golden **74**
bishops 75
   see also bishop
blackbird
   Red-breasted **66**
   Red-winged **66**
   Rusty **66**
   Yellow-headed **67**
blackbirds 66
   American 66-67
   see also blackbird, bobolink, cowbirds, grackles, oropendulas
bobolink **66**
bowerbird
   Adelbert 81
   Archbold's 81
   Satin 80, **81**
   Spotted **81**
bowerbirds 80-81
   see also bowerbird, gardener
brambling 70
budgerigar **35**
budgerigars 35
   see also budgerigar
bulbul
   Black **56**
   Black-headed **57**
   Red-vented **56**
   Red-whiskered **56**, **57**
bulbuls 56-57
   see also bulbul, greenbuls
bullfinch 69
bunting
   Corn **61**
   Rainbow **62**
buntings 60-65
   true 60
   see also bunting, cardinal,

chlorophonias, dacnises, euphonias, flower-piercers, grassquits, finches, grosbeaks, honeycreepers, longspurs, saltators, sparrows, swallow-tanager, tanagers
bustard
   Australian **28**
   Great **28**
   Kori **29**
   Little **29**
   Nubian 28
bustards 28-29
   see also bustard, houbara, korhaan

calfbird **54**
calyptura
   Kinglet 54
capercaillie **22**, 24
cardinal 60, 61, **64**
cassowaries 12-13
   see also cassowary
cassowary
   Double-wattled *see* Southern
   One-wattled **13**
   Southern 12, **13**
chaffinch **68**, 69
chicken
   Prairie **22**
chlorophonias 60
chough **87**
chukar **17**
cockatoo
   Galah 39
   Gang-gang 39
   Great black 38, **39**
   Palm *see* cockatoo, Great black
   Rose **39**
   Slender-billed **39**
   Sulfur-crested **39**
   White-tailed 39
   Yellow-tailed **39**
cockatoos 38-39
   see also cockatoo
cock-of-the-rock
   Guianan 54
   Peruvian **54**
conure
   Austral 34
   Patagonian 36
coquette
   Frilled **43**
cordon bleu
   Blue-capped **73**
cordon bleus 73
   see also cordon bleu
cotinga
   Pompadour **54**
   Swallow-tailed **54**
   White-cheeked 54
cotingas 54-55
   see also bellbirds, calfbird, calyptura, cock-of-the-rock, cotinga, tityra, umbrellabirds

cowbird
   Bay-winged 67
   Screaming 67
cowbirds 66, 67
   see also cowbird
crossbill
   Parrot **69**
   Two-barred **69**
crossbills 68
   see also crossbill
crow
   Carrion **89**
   Pied **88**
crows 86-89
   see also chough, crow, jackdaw, jays, magpies, nutcrackers, raven, rook

dacnises 60, 65
dove
   Collared 30
   Rock **30**
   Spotted **30**
   Turtle **31**

emeralds 44
emu 10-11
euphonias 60

finch
   Bengalese **72**, 73
   Blue-faced parrot **72**
   Gouldian 72, **73**
   Large cactus **64**
   Laysan **70**
   Nihoa 70
   Plush-capped **61**, 62
   Sharp-beaked ground **64**
   Small ground **64**
   Vegetarian **64**
   Warbler **64**
   Woodpecker **64**
   Zebra **72**, 73
finches 60, 65, 68-71
   Galapagos 62, 64
   Hawaiian 68, 70
   snow 76
   see also apapane, brambling, bullfinch, chaffinch, crossbills, goldfinch, greenfinch, hawfinch, linnet, ou, siskin
firefinches 73
flower-piercers 60
fowl
   Common scrub 26
   Crested guinea **27**
   guinea 26-27
   jungle 16, 17, 20
   Mallee **26**
   Red jungle 20
fowls 18, 20
   see also fowl
francolins 16, 18

gardener
   MacGregor's 80
   Striped 80
   Vogelkop 80, 81

goldfinch
   American **69**
   European **69**
grackle
   Common **66**
grackles 66
   see also grackle
grassquits 60
greenbuls 56
greenfinch 69
grosbeak
   Rose-breasted **61**
grosbeaks 60
   cardinal 60, 61
   see also grosbeak
grouse 22-25
   Black **22**
   Blue 24
   Hazel 24
   Red 24
   Ruffed 24
   Sage 22, **24**
   Spruce 24
guinea fowl *see* fowl, guinea

hawfinch **69**
helmetcrest
   Bearded **43**
hermit
   Long-tailed **42**
hermits 44
   see also hermit
honeycreeper
   Laysan 70
   Red-legged **61**, **62**
honeycreepers 60, 61, 68
   see also honeycreeper
hornbill
   Great **46**
   Helmeted **46**
   Rhinoceros **46**
   Southern ground **47**
   Von der Decken's **46**
   Yellow-billed **47**
hornbills 46-47
   forest 47
   ground 47
   see also hornbill
houbara **28**
hummingbird
   Bee **43**
   Broad-billed **44**
   Giant **42**
   Ruby-topaz **43**
   Sword-billed **43**, 44
hummingbirds 42-45
   see also coquette, emeralds, helmetcrest, hermits, hummingbird, sicklebills, spatuletail, sunbeams, woodstar
hypocolius
   Gray 58, 59

jackdaw **87**, 89
jay
   European 86, **87**, 89
   Gray 86

Scrub 89
Steller's **87**
jays 86, 88
see also jay

kakapo 36
kea 36, **37**
kiwi
Brown **14**
kiwis 14-15
see also kiwi
korhaan
Black **28**

linnet 69
longspur
Lapland **62**
longspurs 60
see also longspur
lories 37
see also lory
lorikeet
Rainbow **34**, 35, **37**
Scaly-breasted **34**
lorikeets 37
see also lorikeet
lory
Black-capped **37**
lovebird
Fischer's **34**, **37**
lovebirds 35, 37
see also lovebird

macaw
Blue-and-yellow **40**
Green-winged **41**
Hyacinth **41**
Lear's **41**
Red-and-green *see* macaw,
Green-winged
Red-and-yellow *see* macaw,
Scarlet
Scarlet 40, **41**
macaws 40-41
see also macaw
magpie **87**
Azure-winged **88**
Green **87**, 89
Red-billed blue **87**
magpies 86
see also magpie
manakin
Blue-backed **53**
Cirrhate **52**
Golden-headed **52**
Gould's **52**
Lance-tailed **52**
Long-tailed **52**
Red-capped **53**
Wire-tailed 53
manakins 52-53
see also manakin
manucodes 84
megapodes 26
munia
White-backed *see* finch,
Bengalese
mynah
Common **79**

Hill **78**, 79
Rothschild's **78**
nutcracker
Clark's 88
European **87**, 88
nutcrackers 88, 89
see also nutcracker

oropendulas 66
ostrich 6-7
ou 69
oxpecker
Red-billed **78**
oxpeckers 79
see also oxpecker

parakeet
Carolina 34
Monk 36
parakeets 34-37
see also parakeet
parrot
African gray 35
Australian king **35**
Blue-crowned hanging
37
Eclectus **37**
Golden-shouldered **36**
Great-billed **34**
Ground 36
Red-capped **37**
parrotlet
Green-rumped **37**
parrotlets 35
see also parrotlet
parrots 34-37
pygmy 37
see also amazons,
budgerigar, conure,
kakapo, kea, lorikeet, lory,
lovebird, parakeets, parrot,
parrotlet, rosella
partridge
Red-legged 20
partridges 16, 18, 20
see also partridge
passerine 86
peacock 16, 17, **19**, 20
phainopepla **59**
pheasant
Blood 20
Common 20
Golden 18, **19**
Himalayan monal 16, **20**
Lady Amherst's **17**
pheasants 16-21
see also argus, Crested;
chukar; fowls; francolins;
partridges; peacock;
quails; snowcocks
pigeon
Feral *see* dove, Rock
Passenger 31
Victoria crowned **31**
Wood 30
pigeons 30-31
see also dove, pigeon
ptarmigan 22, 23
White-tailed **23**

quail
Bobwhite **17**
Chinese painted 16
Common **17**
Mountain **17**, 20
quails 16-21
see also quail
quelea
Red-billed **74**, 76

ratites 6, 14
see also cassowaries, emus,
kiwis, ostrich, rheas
raven 86, **87**
White-necked **87**
rhea
Common 8, **9**
Darwin's **9**
Gray *see* rhea, Common
rheas 8-9
see also rhea
riflebird
Magnificent **83**
riflebirds 84
see also riflebird
rook 86, **88**, 89
rosella
Crimson 37

saltator
Buff-throated **61**
saltators 60, 65
see also saltator
sandgrouse 32-33
Namaqua **32**
Pin-tailed **32**
Spotted 32
sicklebill
White-tipped **43**
sicklebills 43, 84
see also sicklebill
silky-flycatchers 59
siskin **69**
snowcocks 20
sparrow
American tree 60
House **74**, 76
Tree 76
White-throated **61**
Yellow-throated 76
sparrows
rock 76
tree 60, 76
see also sparrow
spatuletail
Marvellous **42**
starling
European 78, **79**
Thin-billed chestnut-winged 78
Wattled 78
starlings 78-79
see also mynah, oxpeckers,
starling
sunbeams 44
swallow-tanager **61**, 62

tanager
Azure-rumped 65
Rose-breasted thrush **61**

tanagers 60-65
thrush 60
see also tanager
tityra
Masked **54**
toucan
Black-billed mountain
48
Channel-billed **48**
Chestnut-mandibled
48
Cuvier's **51**
Toco **48**, **50**
toucanet
Emerald **48**
Guianan **48**
Saffron **48**
Yellow-browed **51**
toucanets 50
see also toucanet
toucans 48-51
mountain 50
see also aracaris, toucan,
toucanets
turkey
Brush **26**
Common 26, **27**
turkeys 26-27
see also turkey

umbrellabirds 54

waxbill **72**
Violet-eared **72**
waxbills 72-73
see also cordon bleus, finch,
firefinches, waxbill
waxwing
Bohemian 58
Cedar **58**
Japanese 58
waxwings 58-59
see also hypocolius,
phainopepla, silky-
flycatchers, waxwing
weaver
Baya **76**
Cassin's **76**
Golden palm **74**
Red-headed **76**
Social **74**
Village 74
White-headed buffalo
74
weavers 74-77
buffalo 76
true 75, 76
viduine 76
see also bishops; finches;
snow; quelea; sparrows;
whydahs
whydah
Pin-tailed **74**
whydahs 76
see also whydah
woodstar
Amethyst **43**

Scientific names

The first name of each double-barrel Latin name refers to the *Genus*, the second to the *species*. Single names not in *italic* refer to a family or sub-family and are cross-referenced to the Common name index.

Acanthis cannabina (linnet) 69
Acridotheres tristis (Common mynah) 79
Agapornis fischeri (Fischer's lovebird) 34, 37
Agelaius phoeniceus (Red-winged blackbird) 66
Aglaeactis (sunbeams) 44
Alectoris
  chukar (chukar) 17
  rufa (Red-legged partridge) 20
Alectura lathami (Brush turkey) 26
Alisterus scapularis (Australian king parrot) 35
Amazilia (emeralds) 44
Amazona (amazons) 35
Amblyornis
  inornatus (Vogelkop gardener) 80, 81
  macgregoriae (MacGregor's gardener) 80
  subalaris (Striped gardener) 80
Ampelion stresemanni (White-cheeked cotinga) 54
Anadorhynchus
  hyacinthinus (Hyacinth macaw) 41
  leari (Lear's macaw) 41
Anaplectes rubriceps (Red-headed weaver) 76
Andigena (mountain toucans) 50
  bailloni (Saffron toucanet) 48
  nigrirostris (Black-billed mountain toucan) 48
Aphelocoma coerulescens (Scrub jay) 89
Apterygidae see kiwis
Apteryx australis (Brown kiwi) 14
Ara
  ararauna (Blue-and-yellow macaw) 40
  chloroptera (Green-winged or Red-and-green macaw) 41
  macao (Scarlet or Red-and-yellow macaw) 40, 41
Archboldia papuensis (Archbold's bowerbird) 81
Ardeotis
  australis (Australian bustard) 28
  kori (Kori bustard) 29

Aulacorhynchus (toucanets) 50
  huallagae (Yellow-browed toucanet) 51
  prasinus (Emerald toucanet) 48

Bombycilla
  cedrorum (Cedar waxwing) 58
  garrulus (Bohemian waxwing) 58
  japonica (Japanese waxwing) 58
Bombycillidae *see* waxwings
Bonasa
  bonasia (Hazel grouse) 24
  umbellus (Ruffed grouse) 24
Bubalornithinae *see* weavers, buffalo
Buceros
  bicornis (Great hornbill) 46
  rhinoceros (Rhinoceros hornbill) 46
Bucerotidae *see* hornbills
Bucorvus cafer (Southern ground hornbill) 47
Buphagus erythrorhynchus (Red-billed oxpecker) 78

Cacatua
  galerita (Sulfur-crested cockatoo) 39
  moluccensis (Rose cockatoo) 39
  roseicapilla (Galah cockatoo) 39
  tenuirostris (Slender-billed cockatoo) 39
Calcarius lapponicus (Lapland longspur) 62
Calliphlox amethystina (Amethyst woodstar) 43
Callocephalon fimbriatum (Gang-gang cockatoo) 39
Calyptorhynchus
  baudinii (White-tailed cockatoo) 39
  funereus (Yellow-tailed cockatoo) 39
Calyptura cristata (Kinglet calyptura) 54
Cardinalis cardinalis (cardinal) 60, 61, 64
Carduelis
  carduelis (European goldfinch) 69
  chloris (greenfinch) 69
  tristis (American goldfinch) 69
Casuariidae *see* cassowaries
Casuarius
  casuarius (Southern or Double-wattled cassowary) 12, 13
  unappendiculatus (One-wattled cassowary) 13
Catamblyrhynchus diadema (Plush-capped finch) 61, 62
Centrocercus urophasianus (Sage grouse) 22, 24

Cephalopterus (umbrellabirds) 54
Certhidia
  olivacea (Warbler finch) 64
  pallidus (Woodpecker finch) 64
Chiroxiphia
  lanceolata (Lance-tailed manakin) 52
  linearis (Long-tailed manakin) 52
  pareola (Blue-backed manakin) 53
Chlamydera maculata (Spotted bowerbird) 81
Chlamydotis undulata (houbara) 28
Chrysolampis mosquitus (Ruby-topaz hummingbird) 43
Chrysolophus
  amherstiae (Lady Amherst's pheasant) 17
  pictus (Golden pheasant) 18, 19
Cicinnurus regius (King bird of paradise) 84
Cissa chinensis (Green magpie) 87, 89
Coccothraustes
  coccothraustes (hawfinch) 69
  spinus (siskin) 69
Colinus virginiatus (Bobwhite quail) 17
Columba
  livia (Rock dove or Feral pigeon) 30
  palumbus (Wood pigeon) 30
Columbidae *see* pigeons
Conuropsis carolinensis (Carolina parakeet) 34
Corvidae *see* crows
Corvus
  albicollis (White-necked raven) 87
  albus (Pied crow) 88
  corax (raven) 86, 87
  corone (Carrion crow) 89
  frugilegus (rook) 86, 88, 89
  monedula (jackdaw) 87, 89
Cotingidae *see* cotingas
Coturnix coturnix (Common quail) 17
Creatophora conerea (Wattled starling) 78
Cyanerpes cyaneus (Red-legged honeycreeper) 61, 62
Cyanocitta stelleri (Steller's jay) 87
Cyanopica cyana (Azure-winged magpie) 88
Cynanthus latirostris (Broad-billed hummingbird) 44
Cyanoliseus patagonus (Patagonian conure) 36

Dendragapus
  canadensis (Spruce grouse) 24
  obscurus (Blue grouse) 24
Dinemellia dinemellia (White-headed buffalo weaver) 74
Diphyllodes magnificus (Magnificent bird of paradise) 83
Dolichonyx oryzivorus (bobolink) 66
Dromaius novaehollandiae (emu) 10-11

Eclectus roratus (Eclectus parrot) 37
Ectopistes migratorius (Passenger pigeon) 31
Emberiza calandra (Corn bunting) 61
Emberizidae *see* buntings and tanagers
Emberizinae *see* buntings, true
Enicognathus ferrugineus (Austral conure) 34
Ensifera ensifera (Sword-billed hummingbird) 43, 44
Epimachus (sicklebills) 84
Erythrura
  gouldiae (Gouldian finch) 72, 73
  trichroa (Blue-faced parrot-finch) 72
Estrilda astrild (waxbill) 72
Estrildidae *see* waxbills
Euphagus carolinus (Rusty blackbird) 66
Euplectes (bishops) 75
  afer (Golden bishop) 74
Eupodotis afra (Black korhaan) 28
Eutoxeres (sicklebills) 43
  aquila (White-tipped sicklebill) 43
Excalfactoria chinensis (Chinese painted quail) 16

Forpus passerinus (Green-rumped parrotlet) 37
Fringilla
  coelebs (chaffinch) 68, 69
  montifringilla (brambling) 70
Fringillidae *see* finches

Gallus gallus (Red jungle fowl) 20
Garrulus glandarius (European jay) 86, 87, 89
Geospiza
  conirostris (Large cactus finch) 64
  difficilis (Sharp-beaked ground finch) 64
  fulginosa (Small ground finch) 64
Goura victoria (Victoria crowned pigeon) 31

Gracula religiosa (Hill mynah) 78, 79
Guttera pucherani (Crested guinea fowl) 27

Himatione sanguinea (apapane) 68, 69
Hypocolius ampelinus (Gray hypocolius) 58, 59
Hypsipetes madagascariensis (Black bulbul) 56

Icteridae *see* blackbirds, American
Ithaginis cruentus (Blood pheasant) 20

Lagopus
    lagopus scoticus (Red grouse) 24
    leucurus (White-tailed ptarmigan) 23
Leipoa ocellata (Mallee fowl) 26
Leistes militaris (Red-breasted blackbird) 66
Leucospar rothschildi (Rothschild's mynah) 78
Loddigesia mirabilis (Marvellous spatuletail) 42
Lonchura striata (Bengalese finch or White-backed munia) 72, 73
Lophophorus impejanus (Himalayan monal pheasant) 16, 20
Lophornis magnifica (Frilled coquette) 43
Loriculus galgulus (Blue-crowned hanging parrot) 37
Lorius lory (Black-capped lory) 37
Loxia (crossbills) 68
    leucoptera (Two-barred crossbill) 69
    pytopsittacus (Parrot crossbill) 69
Lyrurus tetrix (Black grouse) 22

Macgregoria pulchra (MacGregor's bird of paradise) 84
Malimbus cassini (Cassin's weaver) 76
Manacus vitellinus (Gould's manakin) 52
Manucodia (manucodes) 84
Megapodiidae *see* guinea fowl and turkeys
Megapodius freycinet (Common scrub fowl) 26
Meleagrididae *see* guinea fowl and turkeys
Meleagris gallopavo (Common turkey) 26, 27
Mellisuga helenae (Bee hummingbird) 43
Melopsittacus undulatus (budgerigar) 35

Molothrus
    badius (Bay-winged cowbird) 67
    rufoaxillaris (Screaming cowbird) 67
Montifringilla (snowfinches) 76
Myihopsitta monachus (Monk parakeet) 36

Neotis nuba (Nubian bustard) 28
Nestor notabilis (kea) 36, 37
Nucifraga
    caryocatactes (European nutcracker) 87, 88
    columbiana (Clark's nutcracker) 88
Numididae *see* guinea fowl and turkeys

Onychognathus tenuirostris (Thin-billed chestnut-winged starling) 78
Oreortyx picta (Mountain quail) 17, 20
Otis tarda (Great bustard) 28
Otitidae *see* bustards
Oxypogon guerinii (Bearded helmetcrest) 43

Paradisaea
    guilielmi (White-plumed bird of paradise) 83
    raggiana (Raggiana bird of paradise) 82, 83
    rudolphi (Blue bird of paradise) 82, 84
Paradisaeidae *see* birds of paradise
Passer
    domesticus (House sparrow) 74, 76
    montanus (Tree sparrow) 76
Passerina leclancherii (Rainbow bunting) 62
Patagona gigas (Giant hummingbird) 42
Pavo cristatus (peacock) 16, 17, 19, 20
Perisoreus canadensis (Gray jay) 86
Perrissocephalus tricolor (calfbird) 54
Petronia (rock sparrows) 76
    xanthocollis (Yellow-throated sparrow) 76
Pezoporus wallicus (Ground parrot) 36
Phaethornis (hermits) 44
    superciliosus (Long-tailed hermit) 42
Phainopepla nitens (phainopepla) 59
Phainoptila (silky-flycatchers) 59
Phasianidae *see* pheasants and quails

Phasianus colchicus (Common pheasant) 20
Pheucticus ludovicianus (Rose-breasted grosbeak) 61
Philabura flavirostris (Swallow-tailed cotinga) 54
Phyllastrephus (greenbuls) 56
Philetairus socius (Social weaver) 74
Pica pica (magpie) 87
Pipra
    erythrocephala (Golden-headed manakin) 52
    filicauda (Wire-tailed manakin) 53
    mentalis (Red-capped manakin) 53
Pipridae *see* manakins
Platycercus elegans (Crimson rosella) 37
Platyspiza crassirostris (Vegetarian finch) 64
Ploceidae *see* weavers
Ploceinae *see* weavers, true
Ploceus
    bojeri (Golden palm weaver) 74
    cucullatus (Village weaver) 74
    philippinus (Baya weaver) 76
Poephila guttata (Zebra finch) 72, 73
Probosciger aterrimus (Great black or Palm cockatoo) 38, 39
Procnias (bellbirds) 54
Psephotus chrysopterygius (Golden-shouldered parrot) 36
Psittacidae *see* cockatoos, macaws, parakeets, parrots
Psittacus erithacus (African gray parrot) 35
Psittirostra psittacea (ou) 69
Pterocles
    alchata (Pin-tailed sandgrouse) 32
    namaqua (Namaqua sandgrouse) 32
    senegallus (Spotted sandgrouse) 32
Pteroclididae *see* sandgrouse
Pterocnemia pennata (Darwin's rhea) 9
Pteroglossus (aracaris) 50, 51
    torquatus (Collared aracari) 48
Ptilogonys (silky-flycatchers) 59
Ptilonorhynchidae *see* bowerbirds
Ptilonorhynchus violaceus (Satin bowerbird) 80, 81
Ptiloris (riflebirds) 84
    magnificus (Magnificent riflebird) 83
Purpureicephalus spurius (Red-capped parrot) 37
Pycnonotidae *see* bulbuls

Pycnonotus
    cafer (Red-vented bulbul) 56
    jocosus (Red-whiskered bulbul) 56, 57
    xanthopygos (Black-headed bulbul) 57
Pyrrhocorax pyrrhocorax (chough) 87
Pyrrhula pyrrhula (bullfinch) 69

Quelea quelea (Red-billed quelea) 74, 76
Quiscalus quiscula (Common grackle) 66

Ramphastos 50
    swainsonii (Chestnut-mandibled toucan) 48
    toco (Toco toucan) 48, 50
    tucanus (Cuvier's toucan) 51
    vitellinus (Channel-billed toucan) 48
Rhea americana (Common or Gray rhea) 8, 9
Rheiidae *see* rheas
Rheinardia ocellata (Crested argus) 16, 20
Rhinoplax vigil (Helmeted hornbill) 46
Rhodinocichla rosea (Rose-breasted thrush tanager) 61
Rupicola
    peruviana (Peruvian cock-of-the-rock) 54
    rupicola (Guianan cock-of-the-rock) 54

Saltator maximus (Buff-throated saltator) 61
Selenidera (toucanets) 50
    culik (Guianan toucanet) 48
Sericulus bakeri (Adelbert bowerbird) 81
Spizella arborea (American tree sparrow) 60
Streptopelia
    chinensis (Spotted dove) 30
    decaocto (Collared dove) 30
    turtur (Turtle dove) 31
Strigops habroptilus (kakapo) 36
Struthio camelus (ostrich) 6-7
Sturnidae *see* starlings
Sturnus vulgaris (European starling) 78, 79

Tangara cabanisi (Azure-rumped tanager) 65
Tanygnathus megalorhynchus (Great-billed parrot) 34
Teleonema filicauda (Cirrhate manakin) 52
Telespyza ultima (Nihoa finch) 70
    cantans (Laysan finch) 70
Tersina viridis (Swallow-tanager) 61, 62
Tetrao urogallus (capercaillie) 22, 24

Tetraogallus (snowcocks) 20
Tetraonidae *see* grouse
Tetrax tetrax (Little bustard) 29
Tityra semifasciata (Masked
   tityra) 54
Tockus
   deckeni (Decken's hornbill)
      46
   flavirostris (Yellow-billed
      hornbill) 47

Trichoglossus
   chlorolepidotus
      (Scaly-breasted lorikeet)
      34
   haematodus (Rainbow
      lorikeet) 34, 35, 37
Trochilidae *see*
   hummingbirds
Tympanuchus cupido (Prairie
   chicken) 22

Uraeginthus
   cyanocephala (Blue-capped
      cordon bleu) 73
   granatinus (Violet-eared
      waxbill) 72
Urocissa erythrorhyncha
   (Red-billed blue magpie) 87

Vidua macroura (Pin-tailed
   whydah) 74

Viduinae *see* weavers, viduine;
   whydahs

Xanthocephalus xanthocephalus
   (Yellow-headed blackbird) 67
Xipholena punicea (Pompadour
   cotinga) 54

Zonotrichia albicollis
   (White-throated sparrow) 61

FURTHER READING

Alexander, R. McNeill (ed) (1986), *The Encyclopedia of Animal
   Biology,* Facts On File, New York.
Berry, R.J. and Hallam, A (eds) (1986), *The Encyclopedia of
   Animal Evolution,* Facts On File, New York.
Blackers, M., Davies, S.J.J.F. and Reilly, P.N. (1984), *The Atlas
   of Australian Birds,* Melbourne University Press, Melbourne.
Bond, J. (1979), *Birds of the West Indies: A Guide to the
   Species of Birds that Inhabit the Greater Antilles, Lesser
   Antilles and Bahama Islands,* Collins, London.
Cramp, S. (1978-85), *Handbook of the Birds of Europe, the
   Middle East and North Africa: The Birds of the Western
   Palearctic,* vols I-IV, Oxford University Press, Oxford.
Farner, D.S., King, J.R. and Parkes, K.C. (1971-83), *Avian
   Biology,* vols I-VII, Academic Press, New York and London.
Farrand, J.J. (1983), *The Audubon Society Master Guide to
   Birding,* 3 vols, Knopf, New York.
Forshaw, J.M., and Cooper, W.T. (1977), *The Birds of Paradise
   and Bower Birds,* Collins, Sydney and London.
Greenwalt, C.H. (1960), *Hummingbirds,* American Museum of
   Natural History, New York.

Harrison, C.J.O. (1978), *A Field Guide to the Nests, Eggs and
   Nestlings of North American Birds,* Collins, London.
Johnsgard, P.A. (1983), *The Grouse of the World,* University of
   Nebraska Press, Lincoln, Nebraska.
Moore, P.D. (ed) (1986), *The Encyclopedia of Animal Ecology,*
   Facts On File, New York.
National Geographic Society (1987), *Field Guide to the Birds
   of North America* (2nd edition), NGS, Washington.
Perrins, C.M. and Middleton, A.L.A. (eds) (1985), *The
   Encyclopedia of Birds,* Facts On File, New York.
Pizzey, G. (1980), *A Field Guide to the Birds of Australia,*
   Collins, Sydney.
Skutch, A.F. (1975), *Parent Birds and their Young,* Texas
   Press, Austin, Texas.
Slater, P.J.B. (ed) (1986), *The Encyclopedia of Animal
   Behavior,* Facts On File, New York.
Tyne, J.van and Berger, A.J. (1976), *Fundamentals of
   Ornithology* (2nd edition), Wiley, New York.

ACKNOWLEDGMENTS

Picture credits

Key: *t* top. *b* bottom. *c* center. *l* left. *r* right.
Abbreviations: A Ardea. AN Agence Nature. ANT Australasian
Nature Transparencies. BCL Bruce Coleman Ltd. FL Frank
Lane Agency. J Jacana. NHPA Natural History Photographic
Agency. SAL Survival Anglia Ltd.

6 Nature Photographers. 9*tl* Tony Morrison. 9*br* FL. 10 AN. 11
S.J. Davies. 13 AN. 15 A. 18-19 Graham Bateman. 19 BCL. 20
A. 21 J. 23*t* William Ervin, Natural Imagery. 23*b* Michael
Fogden. 24-25 SAL. 27*t* ANT/F. Park. 27*b* BCL. 28 A. 29*t* AN.
29*b* BCL. 30 AN. 31 BCL. 32*t* Tony Tilford, Press-Tige
Pictures. 32*b* A. 33 FL. 34 A. 35*t* A.G. Wells. 35*b* ANT. 37 A. 40
Heather Angel, Biofotos. 41 J. 44-45 A. 47 BCL. 48 A. 50 AN.
51 A. 53, 55 AN. 57 BCL. 58 A. 59 BCL. 62*t* A. 62*b* BCL. 63 A.
64 NHPA/R.J. Erwin. 66 BCL. 67, 68 A. 70 BCL. 71
BCL/George Laycock. 73*t* A. 73*b* Nature Photographers. 77 J.
79*t* M.King & M.Read. 79*b*, 81 FL. 82 Frithfoto. 84-85 BCL. 86
J. 87 A. 88*t* Michael Fogden. 88*b*, 89 A.

Artwork credits

Abbreviations: AC Ad Cameron. CTK Chloë Talbot Kelly. DO
Denys Ovenden. IW Ian Willis. LT Laurel Tucker. N/A Norman
Arlott. SM Sean Milne. TB Trevor Boyer.

7*tl* CTK. 7*br*, 8 IW. 9*l* CTK. 12 AC. 13 CTK. 14 AC. 17 DO.
18-19 IW. 22*l* AC. 22*tr*, 26 SM. 28 IW. 33 AC. 36-37 LT. 38-39
DO. 40 LT. 42-43 AC. 43 Jeane Colville. 46 AC. 47 IW. 48-49
NA. 52 AC. 53 IW. 54, 56 AC. 57*t* Jeane Colville. 59 SM. 60-61
LT. 65 TB. 66 AC. 67 IW. 69*t* TB. 69*b* Jeane Colville. 72*c* AC.
72*b*, 74-75 TB. 76, 78 AC. 80 IW. 81, 83, 87 AC. 88 IW